The

FRESH PRINCE

Project

The FRESH PRINCE Project

How *The Fresh Prince of Bel-Air* Remixed America

CHRIS PALMER

ATRIA BOOKS

New York London Toronto Sydney New Delhi

ATRIA
BOOKS

An Imprint of Simon & Schuster, Inc.
1230 Avenue of the Americas
New York, NY 10020

First Atria Books hardcover edition January 2023

ATRIA BOOKS and colophon are trademarks of Simon & Schuster, Inc.

For information about special discounts for bulk purchases, please contact Simon & Schuster Special Sales at 1-866-506-1949 or business@simonandschuster.com.

The Simon & Schuster Speakers Bureau can bring authors to your live event. For more information or to book an event, contact the Simon & Schuster Speakers Bureau at 1-866-248-3049 or visit our website at www.simonspeakers.com.

Interior design by Esther Paradelo

Manufactured in the United States of America

1   3   5   7   9   10   8   6   4   2

Library of Congress Control Number: 2022945548

ISBN 978-1-9821-8517-6
ISBN 978-1-9821-8519-0 (ebook)

For Mom & Dad

CONTENTS

Contents

PROLOGUE

Will stood nervously at the head of the table.

There was so much beauty around him.

Palm trees that grew sideways out of white sand.

A mist that dropped each morning and enveloped their wonderful caravan.

A welcome warm rain that seemed to know when to step aside. And let glorious golden rays touch down wherever they might.

In service of their Technicolor dreams.

At night a soundtrack—waves crashed on rock.

They couldn't have been on a happier errand.

Nothing would steal this safety.

It don't get no better than this.

And they were allowed to take the bathrobes home.

But he knew their lives were about to change.

At the end of the fifth season of *The Fresh Prince of Bel-Air*, Will Smith announced that he'd be taking twenty-five members of the cast and crew to Hawaii—plus significant others—and put them up in a five-star hotel for a week, all on his dime. The Grand Wailea resort in Maui overlooked a clear blue bay where dolphins would pop their curious heads out of the water as gulls sang their morning songs.

Will had planned a dinner for their second day at the resort at the sandy beach oasis. Shelley Jensen, longtime *Fresh Prince* director and determined invitee, struggled on through a combination of too much to drink the night before and a bit of stomach flu. The guests had all split up and spent the preceding day getting massages, riding ATVs, or hitting the links, which is where Shelley found himself, throwing up just before teeing off with Will, who thought the whole thing was hilarious.

The mood was high, the tide was low, and the group felt relaxed. Will took a seat at the head of the table as the food and vino flowed freely. No palate went unsatisfied. No stomach undeserved. À la carte or the entire cart. Their revelry would stretch into the wee hours.

Then Will cleared his throat and stood up. The sound of gentle waves crashed behind him hypnotically like a muted heartbeat.

He fidgeted a bit and swayed unsteadily on the balls of his feet. After nervously careening through a brief unprepared, heartfelt soliloquy, he paused:

". . . next season will be our last on *The Fresh Prince*."

They all knew it was coming. They just hadn't expected the news to arrive in the way it had. Not words floating on soft air from a kind, nervous boy who couldn't make eye contact.

You see, there's no good or easy way to end any show. And definitely not for a show like this one.

But usually it happens in incredibly jarring fashion. Redd Foxx dying on set. Casts returning from lunch only to be relieved of their security cards. Haphazard notes left on dressing room doors. Once Jensen heard workers dismantling a set during rewrites. No one had bothered to tell them to pack their things.

But this was different.

Will felt the full weight of this franchise on his shoulders, and he hated to let people down. This was personal, this was a family he loved, but he knew inside he couldn't separate himself from the decision. Discarded cast and crew were oftentimes treated with no more care than a brown and brittle Christmas tree, needles everywhere, left on the side of the road deep into March. But Will was emotionally invested.

"He was basically giving us a year's notice," Jensen told me. "The show certainly would have been picked up for a seventh season but Will's movie career was taking off. In our business to get a year's notice was unprecedented. No one was expecting to hear that because we weren't thinking that far down the road."

But Will had already released huge hits in *Bad Boys* and *Independence Day,* and was commanding $20 million a picture during breaks from TV filming sessions. He was on the brink of becoming the biggest star in Hollywood yet still wrestled a crisis of conscience about moving on.

This troupe had, after all, saved his life.

Brought him back from the abyss of both creative way-wardness and extreme debt.

But it was more than that.

He fell in love them. With the fight against his insecurity. With the safety of it all. With the promise of what would come.

How do you repay those who had saved your life? He felt connected to the cast. As he would years after. Their very mention could wet his expressive, sad eyes. Stop him in his tracks. Crack his voice.

James Avery, especially, had been more than a senior cast-mate. He was a mentor, a soothing force for an unsure young man every time he pulled Will aside and placed one of his enormous hands on the side of his head.

Will never wanted *The Fresh Prince* to stop. Not the show, but the idea. Because family never does. Tatyana, adopted sister, was set to be wed. Alfonso had lined up a new show. Karyn had just had a baby. What else lay ahead he could not know.

Will, just twenty-five then, played the part and convened the toast quietly.

The main course had arrived.

INTRODUCTION

There was enough nervous energy to go around. Walk-throughs had gone well enough. The actors seemed comfortable with one another. Bonding sessions at Roscoe's Chicken 'N Waffles did wonders for their chemistry.

He thought the script was sound. There was, of course, the customary interference from overbearing network executives, and they were on an unusual schedule, but these things were hard to gauge.

Could he have done more? What, after all, did he know about hip-hop? By his own admission, not much. And who the hell was Will Smith?

Thirty-two-year-old Andy Borowitz, clad in a black dress shirt, his shoulder-length brown hair pulled into a ponytail, stepped out onto the studio floor hoping for a sign.

He took a deep breath.

It was either going to work or it wasn't. As the show's creator, he had the most to lose.

The audience filed into Studio H with a murmuring low

tide, equal parts restlessness and anticipation. It was a sound craved by both actors and crew alike. Rehearsals and table reads behind them, this was the real thing.

"Bring your real energy on the night!" implored James Avery, who played family patriarch Uncle Phil.

His baritone soothed. An accomplished theater actor, he was the show's anchor and go-to sage for inexperienced members of the cast. His dressing room door was always open. One needed only to follow the sounds of John Coltrane or Miles Davis. There was some Charlie Parker, too.

An odd collection of actors and personalities from wide-ranging backgrounds (and varying levels of experience) had gathered here on this early summer night in 1990. It was time to shoot the pilot for *The Fresh Prince of Bel-Air*.

For some it was just a job. For others, a lifeline. They knew not where any of this was bound. In Hollywood, you never did.

This gig, even more than most, didn't have much of a hope. In fact, to call it a pilot was inaccurate. This was a "presentation," to be completed in four days instead of the customary six so the network could save money.

Its star was pop rapper Will Smith, a first-time actor who would lip-sync the other actors' lines during scenes to keep his place. The network put that all aside, instead counting on his boundless energy and infectious likability to deliver something fit for broadcast.

The production borrowed a rickety studio space at Sunset Gower Studios on Melrose Avenue from a canceled soap opera called *Generations* (starring an early-career Vivica A. Fox). If the actors walked too heavily or nudged a wall, it shook— a too-on-the-nose representation of the show's chances at success.

But that was a discussion for another day. There was a job to do.

"Oh, that's beautiful, darling!"

Fastidious costumer Judy Richman's signature line of reinforcement bellowed as she scurried about making last-minute adjustments to hats and blouses.

The actors took their marks.

"Quiet!" the stage manager beckoned.

The audience fell silent.

Borowitz took a slow, deep breath.

He could still go to law school. The LSAT books were still in his closet. Hidden behind sweaters.

But there was no turning back here and now. This was real. But real didn't mean it was going to work.

Action!

Smith burst through the front door and into America's living room.

There was a beat.

Then a back draft of raw energy. He hadn't so much entered the frame as he had exploded.

Born and Raised

The house on Woodcrest Avenue stood proud.

It was in a row of about forty houses and its concrete facade sat just up a dozen steps or so from the sidewalk.

It's where his imagination would rumble, then tumble out of his head and into the world in a jumble of personal, private, funny, and silly machinations that only he knew. And often he kept it that way, sometimes telling only Magicker, his imaginary friend.

The street was lined with mature oak trees whose branches reached out and touched the ones across the way like ancient guardians protecting middle-class serenity.

He can remember the smell of the asphalt after a welcome summer rain tried to cool the center of his West Philadelphia world. Forty children would spill out onto Woodcrest most days. Ice cream trucks, snowplows, double Dutch ropes skipping off the sidewalk, chalk drawings faded by the sun, the plume of someone's sweet cooking wafting on the evening air.

Football games in the street. Yo, out the street here comes a car!

Girls with colorful barrettes in braided hair.

Mommas calling to come home.

The water plug with its glorious geyser.

Hallmarks of an imperfect middle-class oasis in the safest place he had ever known. Even if the AC went out. Or you saw some roaches.

Woodcrest was home. A place to be loved. The touch of Gigi's paper-thin delicate skin. Her smile on his soul for a thousand years. And a thousand more. A place to desperately escape the concrete of Daddio's fists. The unbending iron of his terrifying, drunken will. A place to never leave. So he could protect his little brother, Harry. Always. Soothe his sister Pamela's cries. Forever and more if she wanted.

A place to laugh and dance. Listen to records. Tell jokes. And eat cake on birthdays. And get presents, too.

To rewrite what had not yet happened. So he could always make Caroline smile. The safety of his mother's love was never out of focus. Or in any imminent danger.

Will would do impressions. Wear silly clothes.

Home was a place to disappear from. Or into. For whatever reason. And he could. If only for a moment.

All he had to do was close his eyes.

A sister, Pamela, was already four when Willard Carroll arrived in this world on September 25, 1968. She waited in the living room at Woodcrest with Gigi until they brought him home in the bassinet from the hospital, which was six miles away.

It wasn't quite a sitcom life—at least not like many aired yet back then—but it was pretty nice. Up those weathered concrete steps from the quiet tree-lined street, the three-story middle-class home in Wynnefield was warm and mostly loving, but discipline was paramount.

They piled into the living room on Sundays to watch Ron Jaworski heave bombs to Harold Carmichael as the Eagles played across town at Veterans Stadium, carrying the hopes of cooks, plumbers, and butchers on their bulky shoulder pads only to fumble them away. When the Sixers won the NBA championship in 1983, Will had found a hero in Julius Erving, Dr. J. Will would head to the courts and try, failingly, to hang in the air just as long as the Doctor.

The Smiths were disciplined in action and in finance, reading their incomes surprisingly far through Caroline's count clothing finds for the kids and coupons from the day paper for meat, groceries, and formula.

n his third birthday Willard pulled in quite a haul of cluding a Fisher-Price See 'n Say, which teaches kids fy farm animals, and a set of Lincoln Logs. Willard Sr. living room floor with Will, clad in plaid (a Smith rite pants) and a velour sweater, in front of a large ed stereo, and built little log cabins as the O'Jays he speakers.

"He Who Is Truly Articulate Shuns Profanity"

Willard Carroll Smith Jr.'s bedroom was at the top of the stairs. He had a preternatural ability not to distort the truth but to enact entire realities to escape, to taunt, and to entertain anyone with an ear, willingly or not. To most he was not to be believed.

His juvenile sense of wonderment was a source of both confusion and delight, and it would pour out through fantastic yarns that would almost work if only he could stay in character.

His rousing, throaty laugh could be heard three doors down, they'd say. Caroline, school administrator and moth and Willard, a retired air force vet, raised him blocks the city's center. Caroline was a proud graduate of C Mellon University and would see to it that her chi' as proud of their educations as she was. She qu' a position on the Philadelphia School Distri collar Willard Sr., Daddio to friends, started Arcac, which installed commercial refri

Will's grandmother Gigi, Helen revere women and, no matter how crowd the night before, show u vice at Resurrection Baptist

And, because granny all times.

"He who is truly say. And the boy did li

When he was a little older, Will would tuck a ten-dollar bill in his pocket and ride his bike to Overbrook Pizza on North Sixty-Third for the best cheesesteaks in town. The grease that turned the bag translucent meant you were in the right place. It wasn't long before they knew the floppy-eared kid by name. He would bicker with his brother and occasionally talk back to Caroline—a problem quickly solved by the threat of Willard Sr.'s belt—but seemed to stay free of trouble outside of the expected schoolyard skirmish, a constant of a young boy's life in West Philly.

The outdoor courts at Tustin Rec Center were another refuge for young Will. He would often play pickup ball there, launching feathery rainbow jumpers. It was a spot he would later describe as hallowed grounds where he "got in one little fight and my mom got scared."

But he wasn't good. And not tough like his brother, Harry, either. Athletic ability had not so much betrayed him as it had never arrived in the first place.

His father's grit for manual labor hadn't been passed down, either. Will would sometimes work at the family's refrigeration business but didn't exactly display the aptitude that working-class Philadelphians had developed as a point of pride for generations. On one Saturday while working with his father, the elder Smith tore down a brick wall and told twelve-year-old Will and his nine-year-old brother, Harry, to rebuild it. The boys were aghast at the impossibility of the task, but reluctantly summoned the resolve to clear the rubble and begin brick by agonizingly heavy brick. Another and another until their forearms burned. They would mix cement and carry buckets. Then they began to rebuild. After school. After church. Before dinner. During the rain. It took them a year and a half.

"Now don't ever tell me there's something you can't do," said Willard Sr. upon the wall's completion.

Will had a gift for making just about anyone laugh and a seemingly innate longing for the spotlight. It would take very little for him to unholster his charm—the threat of detention or to earn a smile from a cute girl—earning him the nickname "Prince" from his teachers at Overbrook High. His high, round cheekbones seemed to give him a look of perpetual bemusement, flanked by his wide, directional ears, which looked like a car with its doors open, only adding to his comedic persona. He perfected a bougie girl's accent and the dramatic, over-the-top *Oh no you dih-int* mannerisms of an around-the-way girl. His exaggerated running man employed every muscle in his body to spasm simultaneously, punctuated by a silly, knowing smirk. He called it dumb dancing. Then he would stumble around drunk as if he'd been sucker-punched outside of a liquor store.

My brother you wanna take this outside?!

A real crowd pleaser was affixing the back of his hand to his forehead and fainting with an exasperated scream, which saw him dramatically flop to the floor in shock after a perceived slight.

It killed every time.

His ability to deftly imitate Muhammad Ali, classmates,

Jesse Jackson, teachers, friends, and Billy Dee Williams were go-tos. Sometimes all he had to do was flail his floppy limbs. The daily one-man show that was the origin of his Fresh Prince identity won him waves of adulation from peers.

Sometimes you couldn't tell alter from ego.

Where Will ended and Prince began.

Or if they did at all.

Adding "Fresh" was his idea.

Young Willard did not know it but he was on a collision course with a twenty-year-old rising DJ who would change his life.

"We Had No Idea How Big It Would Be, Not Even a Little Bit"

Jeff Townes made a name for himself lugging his Pioneer 1200 turntables and crates of records to block parties all over his Philadelphia neighborhood, flexing skills honed in the basement of his parents' modest home on Fifty-Seventh and Rodman near Cobbs Creek Park.

Soon he *was* the neighborhood. His distinct style was almost as familiar as the Liberty Bell. Word began to spread of how he could scratch the record behind his back or with his elbow and keep a party going for hours. He would mix Motown with homemade beats. Sugar Hill with Chuck D's booming baritone. Add quick time scratches to Earth, Wind & Fire.

Townes is credited with inventing chirp scratching, which combines the rapid-fire uses of the crossfader. Unlike his musically inclined older brother, Jeff didn't (couldn't) read music so much as feel it.

"Scratching is a percussive instrument," he told the *Philadelphia City Paper* in 2002. "All I did was adapt. I have perfect pitch. Literally. I know the sound of sharps and flats. After that, it's bars and beats, swing or straight, and me in the middle scratch-spinning."

Townes's reputation preceded him. Kids would jump on bikes to flock to his shows. Others came by bus or would simply walk. Aunties and uncles would watch from porches or street corners. Sometimes someone would open up a fire hydrant and draw the ire of the cops, who would break up the party.

Townes would soon graduate to local parks or the YMCA. Eventually his rep landed him on the ballroom circuit and he could be seen spinning most weekend nights at the Wynne Ballroom, on Fifty-Fourth and Wynnefield Avenue.

Just five bucks to get in. Ladies free.

Meanwhile, Will fronted a crew called the Hypnotic MCs, who would traverse downtown Philly looking to make a few bucks rhyming at local house parties. Heck, usually he would do it for free. The adrenaline rush and attention far exceeded the meager dollar amount. One night in August of 1985 he got a hot lead about a block party needing a host.

It paid thirty-five dollars.

Bet, he thought.

Will and Ready Rock C, his childhood best pal who had gained a rep as one of the best up-and-coming beatboxers in Philly, headed over.

Smith's early zest for performance was born out of a desperation to please, derived from a constant need to impress his simultaneously loving and fearsome father. But his method was not born of charity or service but a lean on laughter developed out of the need to keep restless crowds on their toes. The jovial Fresh Prince persona was born.

"I just thought if I could lighten the mood I could keep everybody safe," Smith told *GQ* in October 2021. If he could keep them laughing, maybe he and his mother and his siblings would be spared the beatdowns that could come from anywhere—neighborhood thugs, school bullies, his father.

It was a dark undercurrent to his comedic facade, one Smith would keep hidden for years. He wanted people to dance, smile, and leave exhilarated by what they had seen when they walked out of the sweaty basement party hotboxes he used to hone his skills.

And it was a great way to meet girls. He would twist humorous rhymes and deliver primal, comedic energy as if it were fired from a T-shirt cannon.

The reaction from being onstage, clutching a microphone, knowing people were there to see him, was intoxicating. It had meant to be secondary to the safety his affable personality afforded him. But before long he couldn't get enough. Will would perform anywhere people would have him, often just for gas money.

On a good stretch he could scrape together enough cash—and combine it with the money he made at his summer job at the ice factory—for a trip to the Gallery Mall for a nascent Fresh Prince–worthy wardrobe: sweat suits from Le Coq Sportif, Ellesse, or Sergio Tacchini, capped off by a pair of Filas or Barkleys.

Fellow hip-hop artist Townes had caught wind of Smith's exuberant style and unbridled ambition, but it wasn't until the summer of 1985 that their paths crossed in full. Townes had booked a small gig up the block from Will's house but found himself in a predicament when his MC failed to show.

Smith, who was in attendance, seized the moment.

"He asked if he could get on the mike," said Townes in a 2020 interview. "I said come on up and the chemistry was instant."

Afterward, he told him he had another party the following night.

"What are you doing tomorrow?" asked Townes.

"Nothing," replied Will with a shrug.

The invitation turned into a string of seven or eight consecutive nights of house parties, dank bars, and neighborhood get-togethers. They each knew they had found what they were looking for in a musical collaborator. Said Jeff to the *Philadelphia City Paper* in 2002, "How did he know I was about to bring this record? How did I know his punch line was on the fourth bar and to drop out? Plus, we were the biggest jackasses each other knew."

They were friends who could finish each other's sentences and had interlocking senses of humor that fit like jigsaw pieces. They were musical collaborators with tireless work efforts and lofty goals.

"It was perfect," said Smith. "It was just so natural."

Soon DJ Jazzy Jeff and The Fresh Prince had developed a reputation for throwing packed, raucous, high-energy shows all over Philadelphia. For live shows they added beatboxer Ready Rock C, Smith's friend from the neighborhood. The size of their crowds and venues grew with their reputations. So did the fees they commanded.

The Fresh Prince, just like Willard on Woodcrest, eschewed profanity, misogyny, and felonious hood tales. It was maybe a touch out of step with the mainstream hip-hop vibe of the era (Schoolly D and DJ Code Money ran a harder game in Philly at the time), but parents came out in droves to chaperone children to concerts and drive his record sales.

Their first single, 1985's "Girls Ain't Nothing But Trouble," was a lighthearted, bouncy ode to a healthy distrust for girls. The music video saw a comically frustrated Prince on the run from a jealous boyfriend and walking home in the freezing cold in his underwear after a date had gone awry. Released on Philadelphia-based Word-Up Records, it quickly garnered radio play and won approval from teens and parents alike; the latter apparently could understand the value of music both palatable to kids but not in need of an explicit-lyrics advisory.

Smith was four months shy of his eighteenth birthday and still thirty days from graduation. He dreamed of world-wide tours and the adulation of millions but still had to go to class as cars with boomin' systems drove by Overbrook blasting his teenage anthem. After school he'd screech off in his brand-new cherry red, twenty-thousand-dollar Camaro IROC-Z to Jeff's, then grab some cheesesteaks and get ready for the night's gig.

Its popularity put them on the radar of Def Jam's Russell Simmons and sent them on tour all over the country and even to London.

While in the United Kingdom they decided to make their first record, *Rock the House*. It took two weeks to write, record, and mix the album. Jeff came up with the beats and arrangements and worked in the scratches. Will wrote the lyrics based on how the beats and bass lines resonated with him.

"At night we would go to the studio and put it together," said Jeff. "We were making it up on the spot."

The unexpected success of the record was as refreshing as the seat-of-your-pants production sessions.

"We had no idea how big it would be, not even a little bit," Jeff told VladTV in 2020. "If my friends heard it and liked it that's cool."

By 1987, life was as sweet as it could possibly be for DJ Jazzy Jeff and The Fresh Prince. They were the toast of hip-hop. Their album *I'm The Rapper, He's the DJ* spawned the smash hit "Parents Just Don't Understand," which topped out at No. 12 on the Billboard Hot 100 list and earned Smith the first-ever hip-hop Grammy.

A month before he even graduated from high school, Will Smith had a hit single in constant rotation on the radio. The possibilities were endless. Until they weren't.

"Basically, It Went Double Plastic"

Mainstream hip-hop was in its infancy and abided by clearly demarcated lines that separated specific genres—gangsta, conscious, and pop—never meant to be cross-pollinated.

As hip-hop's novelty began to give way to a legitimate art form, finicky listeners' tastes jumped from one hot thing to the next. There was a demand for authenticity, hood tales, and grit, which boosted the street cred—real or imagined—of both the artist and listener.

Bubblegum rappers were tossed into the ash bin of irrelevance. Too safe. Too catchy. Too everything. Too nothing. And that's how the G-rated persona created by Will Smith, this goofy one-note MC, again found himself on the outside looking in.

Public Enemy were hard-driving revolutionaries whose thundering music railed against police brutality, systemic inequality, and the prison industrial complex, themes that perfectly dovetailed with the ambitions and philosophy of fellow Long Island native Spike Lee. The three contemporaries—one duo, one director—played off against each other to build their credibility and aesthetics in music videos and photo spreads.

Around the same time, Rakim, Kool G Rap, and Big Daddy Kane ushered in an era of cutting-edge lyricism, with songs tied heavily to authenticity, survival, and an almost romanticized street savvy. Artists cultivated tough exteriors with razor-sharp, unbending stories of hopelessness while never straying too far from the original, South Bronx hip-hop ethos—move the crowd. These MCs rarely showed emotion and never smiled.

Then a tsunami of gangsta rap barreled in from the West Coast in all-black gear, Chuck Taylors, and Raiders hats. Striking imagery—AK-47s and sawed-off shotguns—with lyrics to match would give birth to the PARENTAL ADVISORY sticker for explicit lyrics.

Fuck the police comin' straight from the underground
A young nigga got it bad 'cause I'm brown

There were stories of violence, poverty, and retribution against police officers. Listeners with East Coast, suburban sensibilities could almost scarcely comprehend the shocking lyrics and the velocity with which it was served up.

Bubblegum rap was simply not going to do it.

But Smith held firm. He doubled down on his third effort. More fun. More silly. More everything that made *He's the DJ, I'm the Rapper* a smash.

The result, his third studio album, *And in This Corner. . .*, flopped. His and Jazzy Jeff's almost epic lack of focus did not help. They had dashed off to the Bahamas to record, Smith's first visit to the legendary Compass Point Studios in Nassau, where Mick Jagger and David Bowie had laid down some of their most iconic hits.

Smith had booked three weeks to complete the album but instead took a vacation while burning through "$10,000 a day on rum punch and chicken fingers" for twenty of his closest friends. After two weeks they had yet to record a single song and were $300,000 in the hole.

Upon returning to Philly they had three weeks to put together a listless, tired, directionless album of the kind of music people had become tired of. Its lone memorable song was "I Think I Can Beat Mike Tyson," a comically infused ditty where a delusional Smith attempts exactly what the title suggests. The video starred Tyson and a then-unknown Chris Rock and the song reached a tepid 58 on the Billboard Hot 100.

"Basically, it went double plastic," Smith recalled of *And in This Corner . . .* in a 2018 video on his YouTube channel.

To promote the album the record company put together a hastily prepared, poorly attended promotional tour that cost more money than it earned. Making matters worse, his relationship with Ready Rock C, the unofficial third member of the group, was falling apart in real time. The lyrics remained G-rated, but beatboxing, the Prince had determined, was no longer in style.

They clashed incessantly and nearly came to blows, until C was no longer even invited on stage at all. By the time they returned to Philly their longtime friendship was over.

Jazzy Jeff, defeated and broke, retreated to the safest place he knew—his mother's basement.

(In 2002, Ready Rock sued Smith over claims he is owed $5 million in royalties for the Grammy-winning "Parents Just Don't Understand." "It's a song that I didn't perform on, but I did co-write it," he told the *Boston Globe*. "I've seen a number of performers who made it to stardom, but still took care of their genuine hometown friends. It hurts me to find that Will isn't that type of person." The case was settled without any admission of wrongdoing by Smith.)

For Smith his rap dream was all but over, but fame was still the mission. He had one option left.

Go west.

Straight Outta Shaker Heights

Andy Borowitz grew up in the quiet splendor of Shaker Heights, Ohio, eight miles southeast of Cleveland, raised by his father, Albert, who was a corporate lawyer, author, and collector of true-crime literature, and his mother, Helen, an art historian and museum curator.

There was nothing in his experience to suggest that he'd one day create something as bouncy, cool, and hip as *The Fresh Prince of Bel-Air*.

Borowitz processed his typical teenage angst through whimsy and flights of fancy. The scrawny, self-aware Jewish kid was drawn to parody from the start. His Super 8 movies would often be send-ups of old monster movies like *Frankenstein*. He was a theater kid who was doing plays and improv. He would listen to George Carlin and Richard Pryor records.

The Who, the Allman Brothers Band, and David Bowie flowed from his speakers as his beloved, fruitless Cleveland Browns frittered away glory on the family television set most Sundays.

Cleveland was called the Mistake on the Lake for a reason.

"I was pretty nerdy but at the same time the class clown," said Borowitz. "A bourgeois class clown, to be more accurate."

As a bass baritone, he split his time with two a cappella groups, the Wayfarers and the Chanticleers, which would become the basis for the fictional group the Alagaroos of Bel-Air Academy. Each weekend they would perform at local Cleveland malls to earn money for choir uniforms.

"I felt uniquely qualified to make fun of uncool white kids, having been one," said Borowitz.

Unburdened by the attention of girls, he dove into drawing satirical superhero parody comic books. Picking up a guitar meant at least he could look cool during band class.

"If I can unearth another grievance from my childhood," laughed Borowitz, "my parents weren't sold on the idea of me rocking out and playing power chords."

Acts of quasi-rebellion went largely unnoticed thanks to mom and dad's diminishing zest for extracting discipline from their youngest. Both would be fast sleep when Andy rode his ten-speed home at 2 a.m. after underaged keggers.

"I think they just ran out of parenting juice. I was the third and last child and by high school they were just over it." He wasn't even scolded for denting the bumper of the family car while learning to parallel park.

His parents had been stunned into silence by their second son's dreamy ways, hoping his creative hobbies would eventually give way to loftier pursuits, like a career in corporate law.

Showbiz ambitions were akin to joining the circus. "Be more like your brother!" He had meticulously plotted out a legal career and would follow dad to Harvard. Get a guaranteed paycheck and don't be a financial burden; that was the missive.

As a reed-thin, bookish senior at Shaker Heights High School, he was the editor of the school paper, the *Shakerite*, which often featured comic strips and essays constructed by his own askew imagination and sideways take on school and teenage suburban life.

Shaker Heights ran the gamut of the socioeconomic spectrum as much as Cleveland did. His high school was "about forty percent Black." Many of the kids Borowitz saw every day were more likely to come from working-class families whose parents were mechanics or nurses or bus drivers. But one family was a little more . . . memorable, inspirational: an African American friend's father owned a Jaguar dealership.

"They were kind of like the Banks family of Shaker Heights," said Borowitz.

In 1976, after graduating atop his class, Borowitz packed up his quick wit and penchant for humor and followed his parents' and older brother's footsteps to Harvard. Surrounded by like-minded comedic tricksters, his own seeds began to sprout when he joined the *Harvard Lampoon*—a smart-alecky, student-run comedy magazine—after being pranked by a phony flyer.

The following year he was writing offbeat sketches for the comedic comedy troupe the Hasty Pudding, whose alumni included Oscar-winner Jack Lemmon, Presidents Franklin Delano Roosevelt and John Quincy Adams, and actress Rashida Jones, the daughter of future Borowitz collaborator Quincy Jones.

This was the exact locus of the start of his *Fresh Prince* journey.

In the late 1970s and 1980s, *Lampoon* alumni began to populate writing staffs from late-night talk shows like *The David Letterman Show* to edgy cable television fare such as *Not Necessarily the News* and *It's Garry Shandling's Show* to network sitcoms like *Family Ties*.

"The greatest education I got at Harvard was sitting around the *Lampoon* and watching TV shows and movies and just reacting to it with a lot of funny people," Borowitz recalled. "We really didn't know it at the time but we were preparing ourselves for careers in entertainment. It's not like we were very productive but it was great training in that we were around other funny people trying to one-up each other."

It was there he met Susan Stevenson. He was twenty, she was nineteen. They were drawn to each other's sense of humor, and soon made a habit of movie nights in the *Lampoon* offices and going out for cheap beers. She with her brown, shoulder-length hair and Andy with his weird sweaters.

Susan's suburban upbringing in Cherry Hill, New Jersey, was not all that different from Andy's. In second-grade home-room, her teacher asked each student to stand and tell the class what they wanted to be when they grew up. Nearly every girl announced she wanted to be an actress or a singer.

"I want to be a writer," said the precocious youngster, "because all of these girls are going to need jobs."

She tried her hand at serious poetry but the words seemed to come out in a jumble of silliness. She knew comedy would be her thing. She loved *Saturday Night Live, Mary Hartman, Mary Hartman, The Brady Bunch,* and would never miss *Monty Python's Flying Circus.*

They had both studied English at Harvard, but this was their real education, unsupervised as it was quirky. They could steal away for a night, as college kids do. But their paths were inexorably sealed.

When Andy would eventually leave for Los Angeles, he asked Susan to marry him. He left. She followed a year later.

"Would You Like to Come Out and Work for Me?"

Andy Borowitz's as-yet-undetermined career took a leap toward Hollywood when he asked to introduce a Harvard campus screening of Gene Wilder's *Start the Revolution Without Me.* Producer Bud Yorkin was in town to be honored for the flick, and Andy had spotted an opportunity. Borowitz used his stage time to wing ten minutes of stand-up, managing to

29

get a few laughs in the process. Yorkin got a kick out of the good-natured barbs directed his way and pulled the impetuous host aside afterward.

"You're a funny guy," said Yorkin. "Would you like to come out and work for me?"

Twenty-two-year-old Andy answered, without hesitation, "Absolutely."

Borowitz couldn't believe his stroke of luck. He'd never been much of a risk-taker and knew he didn't have it in him to go to Hollywood and wait tables while hoping for his big break.

In ten minutes his entire life trajectory changed. He canceled fellowship applications and even turned down a couple of solid writing offers in New York. Now it was time to tell his father he wasn't going to become a lawyer.

"My parents were kind of stuck in the nineteenth century," said Borowitz. "They just didn't see writing as a viable career path. They didn't think it was real. Their great fear was that I would be stuck somewhere unable to make a living."

Senior thesis completed (on comedy writing in the seventeenth-century Restoration period), he bought a plane ticket and was off to Los Angeles.

There he joined Yorkin in his efforts to try to get several screenplays produced. It was a pursuit he quickly found slow, monotonous, and not all that fun. Yorkin's secretary asked him if he'd prefer a shot at writing on an existing show, as opposed to developing screenplays that seemed to go nowhere.

He was offered a three-year deal with Yorkin's Embassy Television. In 1981 he jumped at the chance and landed a staff writing job on *Archie Bunker's Place*, a placid follow-up to the Norman Lear–produced smash *All in the Family*.

"The show doesn't hold up today," laughed Borowitz. "But it wasn't very good back then, either."

He was working, at least, but Borowitz's isolation and loneliness on the West Coast seemed all-consuming. He was three thousand miles away from home and didn't know anybody. Susan was still a year away from graduation and they struggled to navigate the time difference.

He lived alone in a spartan studio apartment at 212 Reeves Drive in what was affectionately referred to as the "slums" of Beverly Hills—garden-variety apartments with majestic names, typically south of Wilshire Boulevard. He outfitted the place with a rust-colored futon sofa. A table sat in the corner with space for no more than a typewriter. This being LA, he next invested in a set of wheels . . . a used bicycle he found in the classified ads for thirty-five dollars and which he used to ferry himself to the office three miles away in Century City.

During the second year of his deal he moved to the writing staff of a short-lived comedy called *Square Pegs*, starring an unknown Sarah Jessica Parker. With hindsight, it unofficially served as an early template for Judd Apatow's totemic sitcom *Freaks and Geeks*, but in its time CBS hung on for just twenty mostly forgotten episodes.

From there he scored a gig on one of the longest-running sitcoms of the 1980s, the popular sitcom *The Facts of Life*, where he penned five episodes of the hit show about an all-girl boarding school in Peekskill, New York.

"It was exactly the type of show that I would never watch," recalled Borowitz. "I never bought into the preachiness of the show. I couldn't get into it."

Borowitz quickly realized he'd fallen out of favor with the show's writers and producers and felt resented. The feeling was mutual. He'd intentionally write jokes he knew they'd turn down. He was frozen out at a cast party. He knew this wasn't sustainable. And then there was his relationship with Yorkin.

The dynamic between Borowitz and Yorkin had taken a peculiar turn after its hopeful beginning. Despite his talent and vision, Yorkin was in an unenviable stage in his life—mid-fifties, going through a grueling divorce, and perpetually crotchety. Borowitz saw this model of what he thought to be success in the flesh struggling with his creative and personal futures, and the collateral damage was on the verge of claiming his sanity.

On trips to Yorkin's Bel-Air megamansion he'd see his friend unhappily sitting in a living room "the size of an airport hangar." Borowitz began to doubt the wisdom of his show business folly. Just like his parents had warned. He had never taken a screenwriting class. He didn't have a mentor of any kind. His sense of career insecurity, coupled with the isolation, left him constantly on the brink of throwing in the towel.

He checked on the Law School Admissions Test practice books stowed away in the back of his closet, just in case.

In 1985, with his deal up at Lear and Yorkin's Embassy Television, he began to field offers. It was the fresh start he insisted he needed. He put his contacts to use.

Then came the writers' strike of 1988.

With pencils down, Borowitz had trouble filling the hours. He picked up his guitar and joined a garage band, the G Scene. Future *King of Queens* creator Michael Weithorn was the bassist, while the film director Marc Lawrence (Hugh Grant fans would know him from *Two Weeks Notice*) handled drums. Their ringer was lead singer Michael J. Fox, who was starring in the mega-successful Back to the Future franchise at the time. Fox thrilled dozens of basement gig attendees with his woefully out-of-tune, red maple leaf emblazoned guitar. He wasn't exactly Chuck Berry (or even Marty McFly playacting at Chuck Berry) but sparse audiences of friends and other unemployed writers got a kick nonetheless.

Then Borowitz got a phone call that would change his life.

The chairman of NBC was on the other end of the line. Brandon Tartikoff was calling to say he was canceling *Day by Day*, a fledgling series Borowitz was working on that was created by Gary David Goldberg and was set to star a fresh young actress named Julia Louis-Dreyfus. (She would win the role of Elaine on *Seinfeld* only months later.)

"But," Tartikoff said, "I really want to keep you."

The brash and energetic Tartikoff was just thirty-four and on a meteoric rise. He had almost single-handedly saved the struggling network with massive hits like *The Cosby Show* and *Family Ties*. He had doggedly pursued Bill Cosby to write a pilot, cast Michael J. Fox on *Family Ties*, and most recently saved *Seinfeld* from a swift cancellation.

Back then hit network shows were owned by other entities—Paramount owned *Cheers* while Warner claimed *The Cosby Show*. NBC was trying to get into the ownership game. A myriad of antitrust regulations kept the networks from producing their own shows. But the rules were changing. Companies were becoming vertically integrated conglomerates and owning and producing all of their own programming.

Gone were the financial syndication rules—colloquially know as Fin Syn Rules—which now meant that NBC could own a certain percentage of their schedule. All bets were off.

"Every studio in town was after the next *Cosby* or *Cheers*," Borowitz recalled to me. "That was the game at the time so I ended up signing an overall deal with NBC Productions."

Four years earlier, Susan had gotten a job on the writing staff at *Family Ties*, which was winding down just around the time Tartikoff phoned Andy.

The shows ended around the same time and Andy and Susan were contemplating working together.

"I didn't know if it was the right time," said Susan, "because he had run shows and I had not."

They had just had their first daughter, Alexandra.

"So we thought that this is better because if there's an emergency," recalled Susan, "one of us could handle the show and the other could go to a squeaky clarinet concert."

"We had a very profitable, friendly, fruitful relationship

with Brandon Tartikoff and we liked that the guy who was running the show also handled the schedule."

"We Were Selling Joints and Red Devils"

He dreamed about living in the Hollywood Hills and making deals. Not down here where it was crowded and bumping into someone could lead to a fight that could change the course of your life. He wanted a lofty view like the ones he saw in magazines and old Hollywood movies. But those were pipe dreams for an introverted eight-year-old with a single pair of shoes and little else.

Benny Medina grew up in a run-down neighborhood in Watts, in East Los Angeles, with four brothers and sisters. When he was eight his world shattered. His beloved mother succumbed to cancer and his father, Benny, who had faded in and out of his life, faded mostly for good. Benny Jr. was put in a series of foster homes but remembered the first most vividly.

"My earliest childhood memory is a green room," he recalled in an interview with *Ebony* magazine in 1992. "That was the color of the walls in the home I was put when my mother died."

Benny Sr. was born just outside Dallas and split his time between Los Angeles and the Fort Worth area. At an early age he fell in love with jazz and would pick up jobs in the rhythm and percussion sections of various jazz bands to afford food and maintain his instruments. He often sold marijuana, speed, and heroin, which saw him rotate in and out of prison for much of his son's young life.

In 1972, at a stint in the Wynne Unit prison in Huntsville, Texas, he played jazz drums in a prison band called The Outlaws. Their resulting country record, *Behind the Walls*, was often sold at local rodeos and even got airplay.

Withdrawn and depressed, the younger Medina would sit in his room just staring at the walls. After he had run away from no fewer than five foster homes in two years, his aunt took in Medina and his siblings. Seven of them crammed into a three-room house, where he slept on the couch in the living room. He was happy to be back living with relatives and not neglectful strangers, but a new problem arose. Medina claimed he was routinely beaten by his aunt's new short-tempered husband (although no formal complaint was ever made). A broom handle and an extension cord were his weapons of choice.

Rozzell Sykes claimed that was just his tough love brand of discipline, for Benny's benefit because he lacked a father figure. To escape, Medina fell in with a tough crowd and hung out at all hours to avoid coming home.

"We were selling joints and Red Devils," said Medina. They would cruise Central Avenue and 103rd Street looking to score and deal. But Benny wanted to try something new. His entrepreneurial spirit showed even at twelve years old. He and his friends began throwing house parties, complete with rum punch and booze.

They'd pocket some cash and it kept Medina from having to go home. But one by one, and with alarming frequency, his friends fell victim to the streets. One was shot in the back; another got twenty years for assault with a deadly weapon. It was around this time that Medina began hanging out at a community arts center that had programs for children.

One afternoon in 1972, he met a nine-year-old from Beverly Hills named Allen Elliott, who shared his taste in music. They both loved Motown and Chuck Berry. Michael Jackson's "Rockin' Robin" was the jam.

Medina hit it off not only with the boy but with his mother, Bobbi, as well. When she learned his story she offered to let him move in with them in their mansion in Beverly Hills, after confiding that she, too, had had a troubled childhood. After some pushback from her husband, composer Jack Elliott, Medina soon moved twenty-one miles west and a world away from Watts to Beverly Hills and an entirely new life.

He stayed in the newly remodeled pool house and enrolled in exclusive Beverly Hills High School. He was mesmerized that kids his age had access to amenities they took for granted.

"The gym had a swimming pool and the photography class had Nikon cameras," he recalled.

Medina was an instant hit and had little trouble adjusting to his new surroundings. He won the position of starting fullback on the football team and joined the drama club, where he displayed a flair for dramatic acting. He was elected class president as his teachers marveled at his aptitude and thirst for knowledge. He would often stay after class and work on extra-credit projects. And he was making connections.

In his senior year he met the sons of legendary Motown producer Berry Gordy Jr.—Berry IV and Kerry—and made such a strong impression on the music man that he signed Medina to a singing contract in his senior year. But Medina was far more intrigued by the business side of the music business and became Gordy's newest protégé and youngest executive. After graduation Medina moved in with Gordy. He quickly developed a reputation as having an eye for discovering new talent and helping artists develop their sound. He soon began to collaborate with some of Motown's top acts, including the Temptations and Smokey Robinson.

Six years later Medina jumped to Warner Bros. Records, becoming the youngest Black vice president and general manager of urban music in history. He began to help shape the sound of Black music, working with Prince, Babyface, Naughty by Nature, and Queen Latifah while racking up twenty-nine gold records and six platinum albums.

Despite his meteoric music success, Medina had an itch he couldn't scratch. He wanted to get into TV and film but couldn't find a suitable story to announce himself to the world as a Hollywood producer. His proximity to Hollywood, thanks to the cross-pollination of the entertainment industry, put him in contact with an endless array of people he could bounce ideas off and learn the ropes.

But nothing quite appealed to him, so he began to look inward at his own life. He always felt he was living a movie, so why not mine his own life? The hardscrabble upbringing. Brushes with the law. Abuse at the hands of others. The transformation his life underwent, going from Watts to Beverly Hills. He knew he had something.

Medina hooked up with friend Jeff Pollack, a University of Southern California film school grad who had just returned from Asia after three years of documenting its small villages, lush jungles, and exotic provinces. Pollack dove into real estate upon his return but wanted to get back to his storytelling roots. With his wavy long black hair and boundless energy, Pollack loved new ideas. Benny's rags-to-riches story was no exception.

They began to develop the idea further, pulling much of it, including broad character archetypes and awkward situations, from Medina's fish-out-of-water experience. But there was one very important adjustment. The wealthy host family would be Black. Viewers had seen two underprivileged Black kids move in with a wealthy family on *Diff'rent Strokes*, which was ending its wildly popular eight-season run on ABC in the mid-1980s as Medina and Pollack were starting to develop their idea. The wisecracking ten-year-old Arnold Jackson's quips, observations, and catchphrase "Watchu talkin' 'bout, Willis?" made him one of the most popular sitcom characters of the 1980s. The character based on Medina would es-

39

sentially be an older version, so his idea needed an updated wrinkle to differentiate itself and get networks interested.

Making the as-yet-unnamed Banks family Black allowed the show "to cover Black-on-Black prejudice as well as class difference," said Medina.

It in effect could broaden the spectrum of how Black people were portrayed and ways they related to one another when coming from different backgrounds, an idea scarcely seen in television before. Typical sitcoms involving Black-centric themes and characters either featured Black people from the same circumstances or highlighted the differences between white and Black people usually with culture clash, wavering beliefs, or economic upbringing.

Through his work at Warner Bros. Records as vice president of urban music, Medina was at the center of the 1980s hip-hop explosion and had access to nearly every act in the business. "Parents Just Don't Understand" had just won the first-ever Grammy Award for Best Rap Performance at the 1989 Grammys at the Shrine Auditorium, an event Medina had attended.

There was something he liked about the bouncy, affable rapper that he thought would be perfect for his show. He was funny, likable, nonthreatening. So what if he didn't act? Who cares if "rapper-turned-actor" was a concept that didn't even exist?

Benny wanted to try something new.

One problem: he'd never met him.

"I Was Poor People *Broke. I Couldn't Afford Gas for My Motorcycle.*"

Will Smith had become irrelevant even faster than he had become famous. He was broke. Stacks of cash turned to lint. Returned calls came about as often as Halley's Comet. And he'd left Philly on a sour note, a horrible breakup ending with Will setting a trash can full of his ex's clothes on fire.

Smith was fresh in Los Angeles and reeling. Manager James Lassiter was back in the bedroom at his mother's house. He and Jazz were on two different wavelengths—the DJ still holed up at his mom's in Philadelphia, just as broke as he was. Jazz didn't even want to *try* to get back on their musical feet.

Will was in for $2.1 million to the Internal Revenue Service, who began to snatch up his cars, motorcycles, stereo equipment, and whatever the hell else wasn't nailed down.

"I had six vehicles," said Smith. "Four cars and two motorcycles and I lined them up out front so Daddio could come see."

Daddio rolled up and got out of his car.

"These all yours?" Daddio asked quizzically.

"Yeah, watchu think?"

"Nigga, you only got one ass, why you need six cars?"

It was a way for him to say, "You blowing your money."

"Uncle Sam agreed," said Will.

The IRS had come calling for real and took with them all six of those rides after he provided all the keys and titles.

And the pool table. When they came for Will's beloved house in Lower Merion, he knew it was the end.

"I wasn't rich people broke," Smith recalled. "Like where you have assets and you just move some things around. I was *poor people* broke. I couldn't afford gas for my motorcycle."

His American Express card was on tilt, so the only way he could get to Los Angeles was to borrow cash from a friend. He had a Grammy but had to approach a gangster, hat in hand, lower his head, and ask for money. The gangster gave him ten thousand dollars in a brown paper bag.

He left for Los Angeles that night.

For the first time in forever he didn't have any real plan to speak of. He couldn't get over the fact that his fame and influence and star power had come crashing to the ground. He had a hard time getting into clubs—silly, maybe, but slights like that were ego-crushing. And his fraying ego was the only thing he had left.

Smith rode the bus across Los Angeles to get to appointments that usually fell through. His career was kaput, but he couldn't hide that diminishingly famous face. Fellow passengers would do a double take and pull out Sharpies. He signed clothing, McDonald's bags, and even babies.

"Being famous and broke sucks," Smith said. "Becoming famous is like the most fun you can have. That ride up is the most fun. Being famous is a little bit of a mixed bag. But unfamous? Post famous? Broke famous? When you used to be hot? It's horrific!"

But he loved Los Angeles for its promise, its pulse, its

buzz. Things felt electric. Plus Tanya was there. On a trip to the University of California, Los Angeles, that previous winter to watch Philly native and Bruins star guard Pooh Richardson carve up Stanford at Pauley Pavilion in Westwood, Richardson had introduced him to Tanya Moore, a sophisticated, streetwise girl who wasn't overwhelmed by Will's brand-name existence—her sister Tgia was dating Richardson, and Will's trust followed implicitly.

"Do You Act at All?"

Tanya helped set up an apartment in Marina del Rey for $1,300 a month. He spent the first few weeks mourning the death of a friend in Philly—who had staked him with the ten thousand dollars—and the rest of the time not looking for a job. If he could pay the IRS back with high scores on *Tecmo Bowl* he'd be straight. But it didn't work like that.

Mostly to get him out of the house, Tanya urged him to drop by *The Arsenio Hall Show*. He felt ridiculous just hanging out when he used to actually be on the show. Seeing all those successful actors, singers, and athletes who might not recognize him was a huge risk to his self-esteem. He worried about coming off as a has-been. But that's what people did . . . they hung out at *Arsenio*. It was a place to be seen and network. You never knew who you would bump into. Maybe anybody. *Prolly* everybody. Plus, Arsenio liked him. And, most important, he had Charlie Mack to make introductions for him. It didn't matter who you were—Diana Ross, Eddie Murphy, Little Richard—if Mack wanted to make an intro it was gonna get done.

So Will decided to go. Objects that stay in motion, right?

He and Charlie began making dozens of trips across town to *Arsenio*, which was taped at Paramount Studios on Melrose. They'd leave Marina del Rey usually about 3:30, if they weren't already in Hollywood, and arrive at 4:30 to chat up any and everybody before the show started at 5:00.

It was there he met Benny Medina for the first time. Smith didn't know who he was, but as a longtime record executive it was Medina's job to know who *he* was. And Medina was a fan. That chat was short. About three minutes, according to Smith.

"I've seen your music videos," Smith recalled Medina saying that evening in late December 1989.

"Do you act at all?" Medina asked.

"Yes," Will quickly replied, knowing he didn't.

Smith has long had a policy that if someone asks him if he can do something, he will just say yes.

"Space shuttle? I got it. You need me to fly it? I'll just be googling it on the way home."

Medina told him he had an idea for a TV show based on his life, about a teenager from the hood who ends up living in Beverly Hills. Will thought it was a cool concept. Nothing more. After all, it was a three-minute meeting. Three minutes in dozens of trips he and Charlie had taken to *Arsenio*.

"I'm stuck in neutral with no way out," says Will. "Everyone's telling me to change my image. Get a new style. Telling me I needed this and that. What I needed was a damn job."

And Will wasn't even sure about this Medina guy. He actually thought he was lying about the TV show idea, which Will still didn't know anything about. But a couple of weeks later Benny called.

He had an idea.

"You gotta meet Q."

"This Will Be like Beverly Hills Cop. Fish Out of Water!"

In February 1990, Andy Borowitz attended one of NBC's weekly production meetings where Brandon Tartikoff, head of NBC Entertainment, would gather all his in-house producers, among them Chris Carter, who would go on to create *The X-Files*, and some guy who produced *Saved by the Bell*. There were a dozen drama producers and a gaggle of TV movie producers.

Borowitz looked around the room and noticed that he was the only comedy producer under contract. This was his opportunity to serve up the next *Cheers*, he thought. After all, he had Tartikoff's ear.

In the hallway during a break Tartikoff approached Borowitz.

"Hey, Andy, have you ever heard of the Fresh Prince?" Tartikoff asked.

"Well, I've heard of Prince," replied Borowitz.

By his own admission Borowitz's knowledge of hip-hip was limited to "the things white people would watch on MTV." In other words he knew nothing. Quincy Jones had an idea for a new show based on music manager Benny Medina's life. And Jones was crazy about twenty-one-year-old Will Smith, whom Benny suggested, despite the fact he had never acted. Jones knew just as much as anyone about new talent. After all, he had produced Michael Jackson's *Off the Wall* and *Thriller*—the best-selling album of all time—and worked with Sidney Poitier and just about every Black talent of note.

"Will Smith could be the next Eddie Murphy!" Tartikoff confidently exclaimed. "This will be like *Beverly Hills Cop*. Fish out of water!"

Tartikoff was the toast of television and it seemed he could do no wrong. At thirty-one, he became the president of NBC Entertainment. He was a wunderkind in a cheap suit who once said, "I want to live in the TV." NBC was last in the ratings. Until he took it to No. 1. Where it remained for a record sixty-eight weeks.

He brought to the network both drama (*Hill Street Blues*) and comedy (*Cheers*, *The Cosby Show*) and signed a deal with a relatively unknown comedian named Jerry Seinfeld, who had an idea for a show about nothing. Once at a pitch meeting with a young producer he scribbled "MTV Cops" on a napkin. It became *Miami Vice*, one of NBC's biggest hits.

On Tartikoff from the *New York Times* in 1997:

Like any politician, he was fiercely competitive but, again, in a 19-year-old sort of way. To him it was all a game. He wanted to win, but he wasn't about macho swagger and wasn't concerned with the usual Hollywood trappings of success. For years he drove a beat-up Volkswagen. And he was so uninterested in how he dressed that for years his wife, Lilly, would have to buy his shoes for him.

Tartikoff was certain he had his next big thing. NBC had once again slid to third in the ratings and fielded a slate of aging comedies. After all, he thought, he'd done it before.

But there was a catch. There's always a catch.

"We want to take this out to the Hudlin brothers first to see if they're interested in creating the series," Tartikoff said of the director duo who had recently scored a hit movie with *House Party*. "If not, we'll come back to you."

Borowitz never found out whether the Hudlins passed or not. All he knew was his agent and NBC began negotiations within the week. Tartikoff offered Borowitz a thirteen-episode commitment. If by chance it wasn't canceled he'd get the other nine through spring. The studio's main goal at the time was to get a show into syndication—that's one hundred episodes—which meant episodes could be sold to run for years in reruns and generate recurring revenue for decades to come. This was a studio's holy grail in the years before the internet and streaming services.

"Quincy Jones is bringing in this young kid, the rapper,

and wants to find a project for him," Tartikoff informed Borowitz. "This is the one. We want to put together a presentation."

Presentation. A dirty word in the TV business. Pilots were usually fully fleshed-out episodes that would set up a series, and on which networks were less likely to skimp on the budget. A *presentation* was something the network would whip up if they weren't one hundred percent sure they wanted to take a flier on it. A *presentation* only ran for eighteen to nineteen minutes rather than the standard twenty-two. This enabled the network to pay everyone less money if it didn't work out.

"Networks being scoundrels, they had found their escape hatch," laughed Borowitz in a phone call recounting the show's ragtag beginnings.

It would star a rapper he'd never heard of, who had never acted before, from a culture he knew nothing about. A presentation? It was closer to a school project.

It didn't even have a name, so they called it *The Fresh Prince Project*.

But Tartikoff knew this was the one! The next Eddie Murphy!

His young producer was not so sure.

The shows Borowitz had worked on had very few Black actors and even fewer writers of color.

"*The Fresh Prince* was not something I sought out," remembered Borowitz. "It was assigned to me and I was terrified. It was a show around Black culture, which I knew very little about."

He was about to learn.

"It's Now or Never"

Medina had eight minutes. He stood in the center of Brandon Tartikoff's office. He took a deep breath and then plunged in. He rattled off a thousand words a minute and could barely contain himself. Quincy sat there with a quizzical look on his face. He didn't even want to look over at Tartikoff.

When Medina finished he was out of breath. Jones waited for the chairman to speak. Tartikoff stood up and extended his hand toward Medina's to shake at the same time he headed straight for the door.

"Cute life," said Tartikoff.

The executive left the room. Medina didn't know what to think. No one did. They sat in the room for another ten minutes trying to break down what had just happened. They had never been in a meeting with Tartikoff before so their guess was as good as anyone's. NBC's Warren Littlefield, Tartikoff's right-hand man and head of prime-time programming, assured Quincy, "That's just the way Brandon is."

(Littlefield liked to brag that he was the only NBC executive who had heard of Will Smith. Not even Tartikoff, who would become Smith's biggest supporter.)

But Tartikoff would need some time to think.

Quincy smiled. He was always up to something.

The next day was March 14, 1990. Quincy Jones's fifty-seventh birthday. He got a call from NBC, then called Medina. Tartikoff loved the concept. And, shockingly, despite not knowing anything about rap, he thought the Will Smith idea could work. It was on.

But like with everything else, there was a catch. Tartikoff wanted Will to audition.

Like soon.

Like tomorrow.

Actually, tonight.

Otherwise the show was off. But it was Quincy's birthday and he was being honored with a Soul Train Lifetime Achievement Award. The birthday party at his house had been planned for months.

And Will was back on the East Coast (he thought . . .).

Perfect.

There was just no way it would work.

"Impossible!" cried Medina.

"It's now or never," said Tartikoff's assistant.

"Is there any other way?" he begged.

Silence on the other end. Medina steeled himself. Let out a breath.

"Okay, now," he replied with a lump in his throat.

3

Who Says No to Quincy Jones?

Does MIT still have that scholarship for me?" The bus routine had been getting old, and Smith was forced to rethink his future. Let's see . . . Money? Zero. Prospects? None. Girlfriend? Fed up.

He knew his rap career had faded beyond recognition, but the trips to *Arsenio* were starting to pay off. He was meeting people; Hollywood people. He had briefly thought about acting before, but didn't know if he had the goods. And back then there were no Chris "Ludacris" Bridges, *8 Mile*, or Ice-T *Law & Order* examples to look to for inspiration. A rapper had never successfully transitioned into acting.

But now Tartikoff's (near) green light, on the condition of meeting Will, sent both panic and dialing fingers into overdrive. Benny Medina was freaking out about getting in touch with Smith and getting him to Los Angeles pronto. When Quincy finally got hold of Will he was in Detroit with Jeff and the rest of the crew doing a couple of shows at Joe Louis Arena to scare up some money. The show wasn't until the following night.

Quincy told Will to get on a plane.

"Tonight," Quincy said.

"I will see you then," replied Will.

Six hours later Will was crawling along Interstate 405 up to Quincy's mansion in Bel-Air in a rental car, kinda wondering who Benny Medina was, why Medina was staking his future on a stranger whose story he didn't really buy in the first place, and what the hell he, Will, was doing.

Will arrived at Quincy's palatial Spanish estate in Bel-Air. His head was spinning and his empty pockets quivered. There was a row of cars he couldn't afford and a full valet.

"There were forty guys wearing red jackets," recalled Will. "It looked like the British were coming."

He was nauseous and beyond nervous and insecure. He had never felt this out of his element. He was having second thoughts but he'd already come too far. The 405 was murder, bro. He just wanted a drink.

He quickly, thankfully, spotted Benny, the dude he wasn't sure about but the only one he knew there, who immediately wanted to take Will to see Quincy, which threw Will's spinning head further into orbit.

There were actors, musicians, athletes, and politicians. Steven Spielberg. Stevie Wonder. Vino and conversation flowed with equal ease. Guests were getting tipsy off both. Quincy was five glasses in, regaling a dozen wide-eyed, famous faces with detailed, dreamy tales from the booth when recording Michael Jackson's *Thriller*.

Quincy stopped midsentence and sprang to his feet when the gangly kid from West Philly entered the room wearing a baggy sweat suit.

"Will!" exclaimed Quincy as if greeting a long-lost friend. This was the first time they had met. Two Grammy winners barreling in diametrically opposed directions. One in the fast lane. One on the shoulder with his hood up and radiator spewing.

But there was a glint in the old cat's eye.

Quincy was friendly, excited, and gregarious and made it known he was happy to meet Smith. Treating him as if he was the one with twenty-seven Grammys. He quickly powered through upbeat small talk, asking a little about his background, and dubbed him "Will from Philly," which was how Jones referred to him several times that night.

Quincy Jones was onto something.

He was always onto something.

His 9,800-square-foot mansion, tucked safely behind twenty-foot hedges, always seemed to be a hub of creative effervescence. On that night in March 1990, Jones held court on his fifty-seventh birthday among a half dozen or so network executives in the great room. There were twenty-seven Grammys on the mantel. A story here, an anecdote there. He had a penchant for storytelling and a lifetime of experiences to match.

There was the time he met a teenage Ray Charles. Did the Chitlin' Circuit with Redd Foxx. Scored Sidney Poitier's *In the Heat of the Night*. Courted Peggy Lipton. Lived in Paris. Sang under the Champs-Élysées every night. Attended his own memorial service, where Marvin Gaye gave the eulogy. Dined with Picasso. Talked civil rights with Dr. Martin Luther King Jr. Cast an unknown reporter named Oprah Winfrey in *The Color Purple*. And don't forget when Michael Jackson unsuccessfully tried to learn to drive during the recording of *Thriller*.

He promised the story of Charles learning to drive another time.

His audience guffawed, then sighed dreamily.

He flashed a ring Frank Sinatra gave him that he never takes off.

Guests mingled in the great room as Charlie Parker's exquisite *Jam Session* flowed from the speakers.

Quincy's voice broke through the gilded oasis.

"We gonna have an audition," said Quincy. "Somebody get Will that script."

Smith thought: *Who the fuck is Will?*

Someone handed him a failed Morris Day pilot script.

He realized: *I'm Will. Oh, damn, that's me.*

"What? Now?" said Will, scanning the room of celebrities and feeling positively naked. "Nah, I can't do that. I'm not ready. Let's set up a meeting for next week."

Will's hesitance was not unexpected. A year before, he had skipped out on an audition for *The Cosby Show* because he didn't think he was ready. He got cold feet again when he was a no-show for *A Different World*, which starred his future wife Jada Pinkett, whom he had not yet met. For all his bravado and bombast, Smith could be wildly unsure of himself and always take the safe way out. He often couldn't find the courage. He didn't want to disappoint himself or others. He didn't want to not be good at something. But mostly he didn't want to fail. But this time, with his IRS debacle and his career stuck in reverse, he didn't really have a choice.

And besides, who says no to Quincy?

Quincy looked at NBC president Brandon Tartikoff to his left. Tartikoff, the man who could say "yes," was in that room for Will. And he'd leave unhappy because of him if Quincy didn't step up. He was flanked by head of prime-time programming Warren Littlefield. Ilene Chaiken, creative director of Quincy's production company, looked on with hopeful eyes.

Will and Quincy retreated to the study. Will was adamant about pushing back the audition.

"Sure, we can set it up next week," Quincy coolly replied to Will. "And then it will get canceled."

"Oh, okay, great. How about three weeks from now?" countered Will.

"Okay," offered Quincy. "Everybody that needs to say yes to this is out there in that living room waiting for you. . . . How about you take ten minutes right now and change your life?"

Will froze, thumbed through the script.

"Fuck it," he said. "I'll be right back."

When Smith reentered the room the entire furniture configuration had been changed. The guests were arranged as an audience. Will took a breath, then transformed into the Fresh Prince before their very eyes—a tussle of ad-libs, physical comedy, boyish charm, and unbridled raw talent.

The room burst into applause. The NBC execs sat, mouths ajar, while others offered whistles of approval. Jones leaned back, a Cheshire cat grin on his face, and watched as Will's aura filled the room and floated to the ceiling. He had found his star. And didn't even have to leave his house.

He bounced up excitedly, quicker than a fifty-seven-year-old man should be able to, and motioned for Tartikoff to get his approval.

"No paralysis through analysis!" shouted Quincy.

As he would a hundred times that night.

Louder each time.

With each copious pour.

Nobody knew what it meant.

Everyone was drunk.

Will from Philly didn't even know.

He just knew he had to get the rental car back.

Quincy poured another glass of wine, a '69 Riesling, if he remembers correctly, which he kept for these moments. Will didn't drink so much. Or at least not like that. Not tonight anyway. But he could have used a drink to settle his nerves.

Quincy hugged Will and began ordering lawyers around to immediately draw up a contract. Jones gathered his attorney and one from NBC and directed them to a limo in the driveway to hammer out a deal on loose-leaf paper as the party continued into the wee hours. He even called a lawyer for Will. The lawyer was at Cedars-Sinai Medical Center, where his daughter had just been born. He came over to Quincy's that night to negotiate Will's deal and remains his lawyer thirty-two years later. The whole time NBC's lawyers were running back and forth from limo to limo. People were making all kinds of calls. Will didn't even know to who.

Numbers and papers were flying from left to right.

Will signed the contract before he left. He could breathe again. He had done it. He had gotten a job. He was on his way back.

"Quincy Was Everything I Expected Him to Be. I Couldn't Even Say Hello."

It was late April and there was very little time and less money. They had to hire a crew, cast the actors, write the pilot, shoot it, build the set, and run a press tour, all by August. Tartikoff planned to put *The Fresh Prince* on the fall schedule in September if the presentation got approval.

The thing hadn't even started and already Borowitz was stressed beyond belief. This wasn't *Square Pegs*. There were huge players involved and skyrocketing expectations despite Will's inexperience. But he had been so good that night at Quincy's, and Tartikoff seemed to grow more excited by the day. And nobody wanted to let Quincy down. You didn't want the distinction of being on a Quincy Jones project that failed.

Soon there was another meeting at Quincy's. This time with the NBC executives, Smith, and the Borowitzes.

The vibe was decidedly different now. There was a fancy dinner, wine, and cigars, but this time it was all business. The execs talked schedule and casting. Will largely stayed out of the way.

I'm from Cleveland so I'm not accustomed to being in such august company, Borowitz thought, looking around Quincy's fantastic study as the executives gathered.

"When I met Will I was blown away," recalled Susan. "He was incredibly smart. He had it. You just wanted to look at him. I just thought this kid is really exciting. And Quincy was everything I expected him to be. I couldn't even say hello," she continued. "He was just talking in bebop. 'Man' this and 'man' that and 'this cat' and 'that cat.' Here I am from Cherry Hill, New Jersey, and I'm sitting in Quincy's house in Bel-Air."

Across the room at a jet-black baby grand piano sat a shy, gangly kid fiddling with the keys. Will Smith did not have to be electric tonight. He didn't have to perform. This time he wasn't nervous. He seemed to be unaware anyone else was in the room. He had already done the hard part. This was now the calm before what would surely be a storm.

He aimlessly tapped the lower keys and ran his fingers between the black and white ivory as if to read the instrument, to understand it.

He pulled the bench in close, dropped his head low, and began to play from memory. Beethoven's "Für Elise," or Bagatelle no. 25 in A Minor, began to softly fill the room. What a strange sight, thought a starstruck Borowitz. He made no judgments of Smith and still he was wrong.

Borowitz couldn't have been more different from his soon-to-be collaborator. He from the quiet hamlet of Shaker Heights, Ohio, Will from West Philadelphia. Born and raised. One cautious and insecure, the other with an ultramagnetic personality that could turn a room on its side. Or sometimes he could be thoughtful and pensive, like tonight.

Their connective tissue was an earnest curiosity, a sincerity, to find what bound them. They secretly wondered what made them more alike than different. They shared the gift of observation, that perceptive ability to find the truth in the most unlikely of places.

At the piano that night in Quincy's opulent room, Borowitz had found his first moment of truth.

On the drive home in the Borowitzes' reliable charcoal gray 1989 Honda Accord, it really started to hit.

"We need to use that," said Susan.

"Yeah, I think you're right," replied Andy.

They fell silent until they reached their small home on a quiet drive, which backed up to a green park in Brentwood. They always talked work at home. It was just a thing. Work, work. Always work. It was an issue that they would meet with dire consequence and ultimately strain their union.

But tonight they allowed themselves the rare treat of

59

being excited. The streetlights and glowing storefront signs passed by the windows of their car. It felt good.

Andy turned the Honda onto Beloit Avenue and soon they were home.

"They Were Expecting Crocodile Dundee and Beverly Hills Cop and Were Quite Taken Aback by the Malcolm X Poster"

Borowitz sat at the head of the writers' room table on the second floor of Sunset Gower Studios on Melrose. To his side, wife of eight years and co-creator Susan. In front of him, a yellow legal pad and set of No. 2 pencils.

The Fresh Prince Project was the only show yet to be completed to vie for a spot in NBC's "Must See" powerhouse prime-time lineup. Things were moving fast. The network loved Will. That meant more pressure on Borowitz. Will disagreed.

"The pressure is on NBC," he said. "If it fails I won't be any worse off."

This would either be lightning in a bottle or broken glass. They had about three days to deliver a completed script. That meant lots of coffee, frayed nerves, Chinese takeout, and late nights.

The concept sounded simple: Will arrives at the Bankses' Bel-Air mansion from Philly and meets the family for the first time. More difficult was finding the right tone and jokes

60

to set up the culture clash, character relationships, personalities, and quirks of each family member. Then the matter of introducing each character in a very short window in the first act. *Most* difficult was the question of just how much hip-hop to inject—this had never been done before. There was no precedent.

So maybe things were not so simple after all.

"Your main goal is just to not fuck everything up," said Borowitz.

At first no one could understand how the Borowitzes could credibly run an all-Black show that required nuance and a wealth of knowledge of Black culture and experience. A 2015 *Time* magazine interview with Susan shed some light:

> [T]here was this [*New York Times*] article that really disturbed me about how being successful in some corners of the American black experience was akin to selling out. It was a really upsetting story because it was like, how do you get out of the poverty, the more violent neighborhoods, if succeeding is considered tantamount to turning your back and becoming white? So I said to Andy, why don't we make it about that? Why don't we make it about how there are all these different ways of being black?

This idea would prove to be groundbreaking for network television. But the Borowitzes knew they weren't experts on the subject.

"We made sure we had a lot of Black writers and Black crew people," Susan said. "We were very open about 'Hey, if we get something wrong, let us know.' How many white writers grew up around so many Black families that they're able to see the nuances?"

(This issue of the show's Black authenticity would surface on more than a few occasions during Season One, as we'll see.)

As writers lobbed ideas, Andy jotted, scribbled, erased, polished, and brushed away eraser dust until the script was in shape enough to deliver it to the network.

"Back then almost all screenwriting was done longhand. Then you would take it somewhere to get it typed up," said Borowitz. "We would take our scripts to a store called Barbara's Place on Melrose to get them typed up by professional typists. It was the dawn of scriptwriting programs but most writers didn't even have computers."

Barbara's Place was once a booming enterprise. The shop would type up hundreds of scripts per week. Andy's *Fresh Prince* script was being worked up in the same place that had handled 1985 Academy Award Best Picture winner, *Out of Africa*, starring Meryl Streep and Robert Redford. The shop barely survived the nine-and-a-half-week writers' strike of 1988 but has long since disappeared from the Hollywood landscape thanks to ubiquitous, affordable, user-friendly writing software.

The punch list of tasks before the Borowitzes and their team of writers seemed to grow with every second. Each member of the Banks family would need to be agreed upon, developed, and introduced with unique, defining characteristics from the moment they appeared on-screen. They needed to show they could grow and develop throughout the run of the series in order to carry the show for years to come.

There were clashes with the higher-ups from the start.

"When we handed in the first draft of the script, the network freaked out," Susan recalled. "They were expecting *Crocodile Dundee* and *Beverly Hills Cop* and were quite taken aback by the Malcolm X poster."

Andy echoed Susan's account. "The network would always go for the broadest and the most derivative thing," he said. "It was kind of dreadful imagining the network's tagline . . . 'He's the streetwise kid from Philadelphia.'"

But that could wait. A show that doesn't get picked up doesn't need a tagline.

As co-executive producer and a creative driving force behind *The Fresh Prince*, Quincy Jones insisted there be two sides to each character—their comedic persona and a counterintuitive element that amplified their humanity and love for one another.

"They must all have duality," Jones was fond of saying.

They had their premise: A streetwise kid from Philly gets sent to live with his wealthy family in Bel-Air with the hope of giving him a better life. Now throw the fish out of water and watch him learn to swim. Add lots of jokes and lessons about life and hope people like it.

Now all Will needed was a family different enough from him to make magic.

Dozens of characters were pitched, shaped, argued about, and scrapped. Character bios were written, rewritten, and rewritten again. How would they dress? How did they talk? Did they get along? Who could they be based on? Would the audience love him and hate her? Would they care? Make sure they're funny!

Everything was on the fly. The staff had no time. They would stay up all night. A character would be cut only to be brought back to life. They'd get it right only to find out the network would say they got it wrong. Maybe there was a good idea in the bottom of the wastepaper basket?

When the dust settled the wounds were still raw and the battlefield that was the writers' room was strewn with dead ideas, battered egos, and comedy carnage.

But there they found the Banks family standing right in front of them with so much hope and promise. An Ivy League–educated aunt and uncle. A square, whitewashed cousin who would be Will's opposite in every way. An older female cousin who cared more about her wardrobe than their Philly-bred visitor's future. Oh, and a butler. And let's make him English.

And they'd all have the last name Banks. A clever play on class and the striving Will character's relationship with utilizing found resources to carve out a better life, right?

Said Susan, "We literally just went through the phone book and tried to find a name that fit well with an educated family."

Since Will would be involved in nearly every story line, with dozens of possible scenarios, chief supporting characters were written with attention focused on each individual's relationship with Will, resonance with audiences, believability, and potential to generate new story lines through several seasons:

CARLTON BANKS

The sixteen-year-old privileged, entitled middle child of the Banks family whose worldview has been shaped by his family's wealth and the security of his exclusive Bel-Air neighborhood. With perfect enunciation, manners, excessively preppy wardrobe, and a healthy disdain for those who lack a country club membership or a trust fund, Carlton is the perfect foil for Will.

Relationship to Will: His short stature and "whiteness" are a constant target and a frequent source of the show's comedy. As Will's complete opposite, Carlton is unapologetic in who he is. Despite lacking Will's charisma, he shows more self-assurance and conviction than his headlining cousin.

Many of Carlton and Will's adventures revolve around chasing girls and trying to one-up each other and prove their worth. Though they serve as the other's foil, they secretly depend on each other. Despite the constant jokes and adversarial coexistence, Will and Carlton have a deep fondness for each other and often learn life's lessons together, creating some of the show's most emotionally raw moments.

Carlton would be vital to the comedic success of the show. It was also the character most contested by the network. Carlton was a privileged, argyle-sweater-wearing, conservative Ivy League hopeful whose sense of self-worth was only equaled by the size of his trust fund.

Will was the supernova, Carlton the square peg. The network executives resented Carlton's squareness and tried to quash the character at every turn. They thought Carlton's nerdiness was a joke at their expense. Carlton, the execs thought, held a mirror up to how people saw them. Juxtaposed with Will, it was all the more glaring.

"They completely missed the point of the character," said Borowitz. "They just didn't understand the dynamics of the show, that in order to have a fish out of water and a culture clash you have to have somebody opposing that force. Carlton was the absolute epitome of everything that Will was not."

PHILIP BANKS

The Banks family patriarch is a rotund Princeton-educated lawyer whose unshakable love for his brood is framed by gentle nurturing and stern admonishment and frequent doses of sage wisdom. Uncle Phil is loosely based on Jones as the ultrasuccessful rock of the family, whose children's pampered upbringing starkly contrasts with his humble origins on the South Side of Chicago, where he encountered bigotry and violence.

Phil walks a fine line, being embarrassed about his meager beginnings as a pig handler in Yamacraw, South Carolina, while trying to instill a sense of pride and self-worth in his children. He toggles between an authoritarian and a pushover. He is the moral compass of the Banks family, possessing empathy, compassion, understanding, and love in great quantities.

Relationship to Will: With his lack of discipline, disdain for authority, and never-ending shenanigans, Will is a constant irritant to Uncle Phil. Despite this, Phil treats Will like a son, granting him every advantage he gives to his own children.

Like Carlton, Uncle Phil is a frequent target of Will's comedic darts, with his girth and baldness being the usual bull's-eyes. Where Uncle Phil differs from Carlton is that he is an authority figure and can be quite tough when Will steps over the line. The show's unique emotional core is the strong relationship between Will and his uncle.

VIVIAN BANKS

The sister to Will's mother, Vy, Aunt Viv is a maternal, supportive female role model to Will. She is often far more lenient when Will's mischief lands him in hot water. Strong-willed as she is feminine, Vivian raises her children to value self-confidence, individuality, and pride.

Relationship to Will: The soother to Will's ego as well as a ready motivator, Viv doles out discipline sparingly. She readily endorses Will's personal expression and encourages creative freedom, from his clothes to his street-centric take on culture. Vivian is often a calming force in the Banks family—but won't hesitate to pull them earrings off—as she balances raising children and her career. She is extremely fond of Will.

HILARY BANKS

The Bankses' eldest daughter and cousin to Will, Hilary is a self-possessed, aloof, dim-witted daddy's girl who cares about appearance, materialism, and social status above all. She falls easily for attractive, successful men willing to stroke her ego.

Hilary is based loosely on one of Jones's daughters and her perception of the world after growing up in a life of privilege. She once called home from summer camp and left a demand on her father Quincy's answering machine.

"Dad, the water sucks here," she complained. "Can you FedEx some Evian?"

Hilary is indifferent to Will, and his embarrassment and failures serve as mild amusement to her. Inspired by her celebrity friends, she aspires to be charitable, as long as she doesn't break a sweat and always has on the "right" outfit.

Relationship to Will: Hilary can hardly be bothered with her cousin and though Will is thoroughly amused by her foibles, he often extends a helping hand and is willing to go to great lengths to ensure Hilary doesn't suffer from her bewildering self-inflicted wounds. Will's fervent ambition to keep Hilary from failure amplifies his unselfishness.

ASHLEY BANKS

The Banks family's youngest daughter. The eleven-year-old has never known a day absent wealth and pampering, yet she is the Bankses' most well-adjusted child. She takes on more extracurricular activities than her age and steams about being coddled. Ashley's perceived vulnerability brings out the protector in everyone.

Relationship to Will: Ashley is the only member of the Banks family who does not judge Will upon his arrival. In return Will is the only member of the household who doesn't treat her like a child and encourages her creativity, much to Uncle Phil's chagrin. Will is incredibly protective of Ashley. Their bond would last throughout the series run.

GEOFFREY BUTLER

Geoffrey is the Bankses' unflappable, servile English butler who attends to every need of each member of the household. His mundane tasks include cooking, laundry, dusting, and more or less any uncommon undertaking to get the Banks children out of one jam or another. He possesses a biting wit, arid sarcasm, and an enduring sense of self-deprecation, which allows him to get through his drab existence. Despite his station Geoffrey is well loved by the Bankses and is considered a member of the family. On rare occasions he out-wardly reciprocates that love.

Relationship to Will: Geoffrey tolerates Will's shenanigans and is a frequent target of his good-natured barbs. Will trusts Geoffrey above all others and often goes to him for advice when not unwittingly reeling him into one of his schemes. As with all of the other Banks children, Geoffrey has a great fondness for Will.

● ● ●

So it was settled. Kind of. Andy Borowitz and the writers had fleshed out the family around Will. Things looked good on paper, they all thought. But character sketches were no guarantee of a working end product. A writer or a producer can construct a character perfectly in his mind, but it's never the same when a human being comes in to read. It can come out flat. Or over-the-top. The actor can lack pathos or carry the wrong energy. Oftentimes a producer might be hearing an actor's voice for the first time. *Not quite how you heard it in your head,* at midnight, while finishing off cold takeout. The actor's timing, delivery, or physical cues might be off. Sometimes it's just not right at all. The producers just aren't connecting with an actor's performance. But sometimes, on those rare and wonderful occasions, it's better than what the writers or producers imagined. Much, much better.

4

Meet the Bankses

Casting began in earnest at NBC in May 1990. Veteran duo Allison Jones and Sally Stiner were given the reins, but everyone had an opinion about who would play which characters. Some wanted big names to help carry the show just in case Will couldn't. Established names were bandied about; someone suggested Nell Carter for Aunt Viv. Others would pull from personal memory—a character actor they saw in an unremarkable film or an old TV show. And of course, there were the unknowns. Fresh faces. Hungry. Infinite in number. Aspiring thespians whose lives consisted of days waitressing or cycling temp jobs between darts around town to one audition after another. A new face could add authenticity to a character, be convincing enough on-screen that viewers would think that's who they were in real life.

But as with everything about this little project, there was very little time.

"I Think We Should Cut the Sister Character"

She waited for the light to turn green. Hands wrapped on the steering wheel, a glint in her brown eyes. She would smash the accelerator, chirp the tires, and hope it didn't fishtail. Karyn Parsons beamed as she guided her 1965 Chevrolet Corvair across Los Angeles's cluttered grid to an endless stream of auditions.

"I loved that car. It was such a cool car but it started to show its age," said Parsons of her beloved Corvair. "I had saved up enough money and I found it on my own, I got it for a really good price." Its white paint job was accented by a bright red interior.

Parsons took pride in her ability to sniff out a good deal. It was a step up from her father's 1972 Chevy Nova, she thought.

What Parson's didn't know at the time was that the Corvair had been labeled the most dangerous car on the road. Its signature flaw was flipping over almost on command. Lawyer and future presidential candidate Ralph Nader's auto safety bestseller *Unsafe at Any Speed* devoted an entire chapter to the Corvair. The book created a national uproar in which Chevrolet ceased production immediately and led Congress to enact the National Traffic and Motor

Vehicle Safety Act. Nevertheless, Karyn would zoom off from stoplights and race all over town from one audition to the next.

Parsons was beach born and raised. The biracial daughter of biracial Santa Monica parents, Parsons was their first, born in 1967. The Parsonses lived on the fringes of California's hippie craze, and sleepy Santa Monica was populated by surf shops, garage rock, and free will. Rough around the edges but full of unfettered creativity, it had not yet been overrun by the superagents and movie producers who make its housing prices damn near unimaginable today.

She went to Santa Monica High School, where she took drama and fostered a "mad crush" on an eleventh grader named Lenny Kravitz. At lunchtime she'd go across the street to one of Lenny's friend's houses and they'd pull out the guitars and jam for an hour. Parsons lived on the top floor of the Ramada Inn across the street. The Parsons set moved often but never out of a five-block radius.

She got a job hostessing at Delmonico's Seafood Grill on Pico Boulevard. Her friends would regularly drop by to chat about commercials and auditions and dream about their futures as movie stars, removed from the pressures of making ends meet. But here, at Delmonico's, a two-hundred-dollar haul was a good night.

"I had done quite a few commercials and I got them all back-to-back-to-back. It was like a whirlwind of jobs. I did a small horror film. I was in an acting workshop and was auditioning like crazy. Running all around town. I'd do an audition, then go feed someone's cat. Then head off for another audition."

There was the McDonald's commercial where she couldn't remember the rapid-fire lines.

The Coca-Cola commercial where she guzzled soda all day with one of the Fly Girls on *In Living Color* and an unknown Don Cheadle. But then her agent called about an audition for a new show called *The Fresh Prince of Bel-Air*.

After about three auditions, producers still weren't sold on Parsons as Hilary, or truthfully, on Hilary at all. The role had been thinly conceived from the outset, in need of polish and an actor's presence that had not yet been considered. Borowitz met with Tartikoff, the chairman of NBC, in his third-floor office in Burbank to discuss.

"I think we should cut the sister character," Tartikoff led. "It seems kind of redundant, doesn't it? What's the point?" Borowitz wanted to hold off, and knew he had a strong card to play before a decision got put through. "Let's see what Quincy thinks," Borowitz said.

Unlikely as it was, both Parsons and Hilary had made the cut. For now. Parsons had beaten the odds to get to this point: the usual Hollywood casting odds, and the odds for this role in particular as well. She had always seen herself as a serious dramatic actor ready to disappear into weighty roles, not play the comic relief. Between *Prince* reads she was simultaneously auditioning for *One False Move*, a gritty thriller written by a young Billy Bob Thornton for director Carl Franklin (*Devil in a Blue Dress*). The whiplash was strong—Thornton's character was a hopeless, drugged-out accessory to murder. Meanwhile, much to Parsons's dismay, the Hilary character had been morphed further and further into an almost cartoonish stereotype of ditzy California living.

Well, I'm not a model type, so how do I fudge this? she thought. But she was professional above all. Karyn snapped out of it, got into character, and drove across town to do the job. This time, for the first time, in front of Mr. Jones himself.

"I was so nervous and excited," Karyn told me. "I wanted so much to make him laugh."

As she began her detached, Valley Girl shtick, Jones slapped his hand on the table and bellowed with laughter almost immediately. Soon the whole room was in an uproar. She had pulled it off.

"I wasn't a comedian," Parsons recalled. "In the room I just committed to the moment. I wasn't trying to be funny. The writers had written great lines."

Parsons gave Hilary focus, and gave the writers something to work with. They could now build upon a persona that Parsons created. Ready or not.

"It's like, be careful what you wish for," said Parsons, "because I wanted the dramatic film."

Doubts or no doubts, the timing was just right. Her beloved death machine, the Corvair that ferried her to auditions, was on its last legs. Karyn had resorted to pleading notes left under a windshield wiper, begging the city not to tow it, but the car was soon confiscated and auctioned off.

A week later she got *The Fresh Prince*.

"I Wouldn't Have Given Me the Job if I Came in and Auditioned the Way That I Auditioned"

"Boy, that kid can dance." That was the usual takeaway when people first encountered Alfonso Ribeiro's fleet feet. When he was just twelve years old, he beat out a thousand other kids for the lead role of Willie in Broadway's *The Tap Dance Kid*, at the Broadhurst Theatre in New York City. The story centers on a ten-year-old kid who dreams not of playing for the Jets or Yankees but rather of a life in tap dance.

"I didn't know how to tap-dance at all," said Ribeiro. "They basically taught me everything as I went along."

The role created an opportunity that would launch him into pop culture consciousness just a few months later.

Alfonso's first brush with fame, *real* fame, made him something of a legend to kids all across America years before the Prince came along. Michael Jackson, the King of Pop, was about to film a Pepsi commercial and needed a kid who could keep up with his iconic dance moves. It would be a true star turn for the lucky winner, to be side by side with the world's most famous man, rolling multiple times a day, all across the world.

Problem was, Alfonso had to fly to Los Angles to shoot the spot during the middle of *The Tap Dance Kid* run. If it came through, the show itself would be in good hands (sixteen-year-old Savion Glover was his understudy), but the production was adamantly opposed and threatened legal action. They floated the idea of an airport showdown between their twelve-year-old lead performer and a team of lawyers determined to keep him in town. But Ribeiro was not swayed. He put his foot down and they were off.

The commercial begins with a city scene, a street filled with kids bopping to "Billie Jean" before we cut to a young Alfonso bursting onto the sidewalk sporting a red "Beat It" jacket, blacked-out aviators, and a familiar pair of loafers. He launches into a perfect Michael Jackson dance routine on his own before MJ and the Jackson 5 join in and they proceed to go through a medley of Jackson's choreography. The excitement swells as kids run from all around to join. The "Pepsi Generation" spot, with its mini Michael *Ribeiro* Jackson, captured the hearts and minds of kids across America.

Intrigue in the young star only grew when an Alabama disc jockey spread a spurious rumor that Alfonso had broken his neck attempting a head spin while on set for the commercial. Others thought the rumor had been started by schoolteachers desperate to discourage kids from joining the break dancing trend during learning hours. Alfonso was fine, of course. No such accident had occurred, but the lies always did have a way of outrunning the truth.

The Associated Press actually hit the wire with a piece cryptically headlined "Broadway Star Not Dead."

Pepsi spokesman Ken Ross was quoted in the article stating, "It's absolutely not true, but it has spread to all corners of the continent."

Forty-eight hours after the commercial aired, *The Tap Dance Kid* was sold out for two months, and the buzz set every casting director in LA on a mission to book Alfonso. After just six months on Broadway he secured a spot on the third season of NBC's hit *Silver Spoons*, alongside heartthrob Ricky Schroeder. Ribeiro would inhabit the role through the 1987 conclusion of the show's run.

This is all to say that, unlike most others in the *Fresh Prince* orbit, Ribeiro had other options. He was sitting on an offer to join *A Different World*, a *Cosby Show* spin-off entering its second season on NBC. He had to choose between an already established show with an exciting cast (Jasmine Guy, Kadeem Hardison, and Sinbad, to name a few) and the still-underbaked *Fresh Prince* presentation, which had every opportunity to fail. But there was something about Carlton he thought he could bring magic to.

"For some reason I connected with this character," Ribeiro told Larry King in 2018. "When I went in I thought, Nobody else is gonna do it this way."

It didn't quite work out that way, as Ribeiro revealed in 2020 on HBO Max's special *The Fresh Prince of Bel-Air Reunion*.

"First of all, you think about how most people do when they go to auditions," he said. "They go to auditions dressed like what they think the character would look like. I'm in an Adidas running tracksuit, which is so not this character," he continued. "I've never been a good auditioner, the acting was bad. . . . Shoot, I wouldn't have given me the job if I came in and auditioned the way that I auditioned. I guess they saw something, but I didn't see it."

Ribeiro auditioned four times, reading with various partners, before he was asked to come back to read a final time
in front of the network and the studio. But he was up against
a rather large obstacle—the network didn't want him. Chief
among those was Brandon Tartikoff's protégé, the newly
hired NBC president Warren Littlefield. He just couldn't
get over how square and nerdy he played the role. Tartikoff
was ambivalent and content to let Littlefield decide, but Ribeiro had supporters in the room as well. Borowitz liked him
and so did the other actors. Quincy thought enough of him
to vote to bring him back each time.

After the fifth audition he won the role and the cast taped
the presentation a couple of weeks later. But Littlefield still
wasn't sold. He ordered a new, fruitless round of auditions to
recast the role. Ribeiro stayed, but the debate raged on.

"The network all through the first season was really on
my ass about Alfonso," Borowitz told me. "They wanted to
fire him multiple times. Their whole view of him was that
he was uncool and stiff and wanted to bring in someone who
was more relaxed and hipper.

"They completely missed the point of the character one
hundred percent. They just didn't get the show. In order to
have a fish out of water and a culture clash you have to have
somebody opposing that force. Carlton was the absolute
epitome of everything Will was not."

(FYI: Carlton was named after Borowitz's Harvard class-
mate Carlton Cuse, who went on to become a showrunner
for *Lost*.)

Despite objections to his casting and persistent questions from above, Carlton was an instant hit with fans. He played the perfect foil to Will. After the taping of the sixth episode of the first season, Littlefield paid a visit to the set. When he saw Ribeiro he pulled him aside.

The president leaned in: "I'm glad that I was wrong."

"I Didn't Know Who He Was. I Didn't Listen to Rap. I Didn't Particularly Care for It."

Growing up in the shadow of the New York Giants, James Avery displayed some talent as a defensive end and pulling guard in high school and won a scholarship to Virginia State College, an historically Black university.

"I had never seen so many beautiful women in my life," said Avery. "Like Baskin-Robbins thirty-one flavors."

With his mind on the ladies and his attention diverted from his schoolwork, Avery quickly lost his scholarship and was excused from the team. It was back to New Jersey, where Avery couldn't shake the guilt from the disappointment he had caused his mother, Florence.

After his gridiron dreams failed, he needed a plan. Problem was, he didn't have one. So he enlisted in the navy, where he would spend four years punctuated by a one-year tour in Vietnam.

"They were drafting for the Marines and the army and if you weren't in school and were eighteen that was the fate that awaited you," recalled Avery in a 2010 interview. "So I joined the navy. It was a good thing I did because two weeks after I was in boot camp a letter came to my mother saying I was drafted into the army. I dodged that bullet."

He was eighteen and stationed on a ship in San Diego. He thought often about the boys his age who were drafted by the army who would never come home. As a seaman recruit, the lowest enlisted rank, with no aspirations of a military career, he would bide his time and wait until his four years were up. Upon his discharge in 1969, Avery decided to stay in San Diego.

For Avery it was a time of experimentation and personal exploration. He became immersed in politics and the arts while surrounding himself with like-minded people.

"My friends looked like the United Nations," Avery told a New York University lecture class in 2007. "People were coming from all over the country and they just wanted to meet new people and do new things."

A self-proclaimed hippie, Avery felt most at peace writing poetry. He took his cues from Black revolutionary poets like Sonia Sanchez but wasn't above crafting words to win the heart of a young woman he admired. He smoked grass and imbibed. All in the name of free love, mind you.

At San Diego City College he began organizing poetry slams and community theater, exciting his taste buds for the arts. One afternoon while smoking some weed on the Quad, Avery was approached by one of his professors, who asked if he would audition for a play. It was a production of *J.B.*, by

Archibald MacLeish, a modern-day retelling of the story of Job. He did. Soon after, he had gotten his first part.

Later, a theater professor at the University of San Diego insisted he play the part of a governor in the play *Day of Absence*, by Douglas Turner Ward, about a town in the South where all the Black people go missing. The white characters were played by Black actors in whiteface in a reverse minstrel show. Avery's booming southern white accent stole the show. He was developing a reputation for his unique portrayals of his characters and started to work regularly at the Old Globe Theatre in San Diego, doing Shakespeare. Then he won a scholarship to the London Academy of Music Drama and Art to study the Bard.

Avery fell in love with theater; he had found what he wanted to do with his life.

"People ask me how can you do the same play six days in a row?" he recalled. "Because you're not doing the same play. Every night it's different. Every night the audience is different. You're different. Every night you make different discoveries. It's a living, breathing thing. The theater is transitory. Whatever magic that is captured that night exists only on that night."

In the summer of 1979, Avery moved in with a navy buddy in the Silver Lake neighborhood of Los Angeles. By day he would create art, play the guitar, and spend endless hours at study. At night he would score weed from a spot in neighboring Echo Park. He was obsessed with acting and wanted to explore different media. He also needed to get paid. As much as he loved the stage, theater actors often lived hand to mouth. For some it was a secondary pursuit. People dropped out all the time. They would get real jobs, move away, or get married.

But Avery *was in it*. He picked up odd jobs here and there but it was only to feed his pursuit. He was a light for others. He befriended people easily. His mammoth proportions and baritone voice could be intimidating before you knew him, but he made people feel safe. If you needed sound advice . . . ask James. But mostly he would just listen. He knew that people sometimes just needed to be heard. That's what his mother, Florence, taught him. So he was always there with a ready ear.

Settled in California, Avery found an agent and began auditioning for small parts in movies several times a week. He landed guest spots on popular network shows like *Newhart*, *The Jeffersons*, and *Hill Street Blues*. He was the crooked cop in *Fletch* who busts Chevy Chase. He once choked Vanessa Williams on-screen. By the late 1980s he had guest-starred in more than thirty television shows. He did his time playing the heavy, the hired muscle, the father figure, and, once, a doctor. Foreshadowing what was to come, he was cast as a judge nearly a dozen times before *The Fresh Prince of Bel-Air*.

By the late 1980s he was a familiar face with casting directors who would often call him based on his body type alone. Having not yet scored a big film role or become a series regular, Avery auditioned as much as he could. Avery had three more scheduled late in the winter of 1990, but they were a few weeks out and his rent was due. He needed to book one of them.

Maybe that untitled pilot starring a rapper.

"I had never heard of Will Smith," Avery recalled in 2008. "I didn't know who he was. I didn't listen to rap. I didn't particularly care for it."

Avery had caught the eye of Lori Openden, head of casting at NBC. She had had a hand in Avery guest-starring on several NBC shows in the mid-1980s, including *Hill Street Blues*, and his spot on *The Jeffersons*, and immediately thought of Avery.

He was called to NBC and after a forty-five-minute wait he entered a large room with a long table that seated seven "very serious-looking guys." And one twenty-one-year-old kid "who didn't look that serious."

"It was like walking into a vacuum that would suck all your energy out," he remembered. "But there was this kid sitting there with his feet up on the table and his hat to the side."

Neither Smith nor Borowitz had ever heard of him. Avery was given a script and then asked to read. He perused the pages and looked over at Will.

"Take your feet off the table and look at me when I'm talking to you," he chided Smith, who readily complied. The room filled with nervous laughter and uneasy energy. Avery was very old-fashioned and put great value in respect for one's elders, regardless of whether or not your name was at the top of the credits. The scene was Uncle Phil and Will's first showdown from the pilot. It was the first time anyone had ever seen Will read from a script.

Avery began to read. His audience was transfixed. He was Uncle Phil. He laid into his nephew.

"You have skewered everything with your flippant shenanigans!" his character boomed.

"Man, I was with you up until skewering," Will coolly replied. The room burst into laughter. Their chemistry was evident within minutes. The executives didn't need to see any more.

"I don't remember anyone else reading besides James," said Borowitz.

Avery set the script down, left the room, and headed home. By the time he made it to his front door there was a call waiting for him.

His agent told him he got the part.

"They Wanted a Lighter-Skinned Woman"

She could act. She could sing. And yeah, she could dance.

She was powerful, yet elegant. And she commanded any room with easy confidence.

It was as if Janet Hubert was made to be poured into the role of Aunt Viv.

But she was no was stranger to adversity. She had spent a lifetime congealing her soul and heart against attacks, slights, and discrimination.

Her mother would warn her to not play in the sun without a hat, fearing her mahogany skin would tan further—small protection against the racial politics of the time.

But Janet would run in the fields collecting mice and frogs anyway. Pretending to be a cowgirl on the American frontier. Even, especially, if the electricity went out.

She wanted to be a dancer. She wanted to be famous. She'd heard about the Juilliard School on TV and in magazines, and decided that's where she needed to be. She left for New York after prom.

When things got hard, Hubert took a job at Dunkin' Donuts to support herself. She cleaned toilets and worked at Amoco Oil for a summer. Hubert ran with a tight crew of Black female theater actors in New York that included Angela Bassett, Jenifer Lewis, and Loretta Devine. They would paint the town if they didn't have rehearsal in the morning. And even if they did. So what?

They would go see Jenifer's one-woman show. Cry on each other's shoulders.

Tell each other that that man didn't know what he had. They'd find support in one another when it didn't exist anywhere else. Laugh, commiserate, pour wine. Their dreams and friendship were a life force.

Black women who had each other's backs.

Round about the mid-1980s, these theater actors, looking to make the jump to more lucrative television careers, split for the West Coast. Bassett and Lewis rented apartments next door to each other on Fountain Avenue in Los

Angeles. Hubert lived nearby. Nearly every day she would drop by her girls' cribs.

Oftentimes they would jump in Bassett's 1987 Jeep and drive around Los Angeles to consignment shops looking for the best deals. Lewis had a sixth sense, it seemed. They were rarely apart in their searches for work and love—often finding rejection and heartbreak.

Lewis was quite the catch and spent this period flexing her empowerment.

"Honey, I was tryna fuck everything that moved," Lewis told me. "Why shouldn't I?"

Hubert wasn't sure she agreed, but she was also not one to abandon her friends. She took pride in lifting their spirits. They went out to lunch and whatever asshole guy that was never mattered again. They depended on each other this way.

They were supposed to be tough. Sexy. Fly. Badass. But they routinely soothed each other's vulnerabilities. In a way that only Black women can do for each other. That they would only reveal to one another. Secrets, pain, insecurities only they knew.

As they began to book jobs, they saw each other less and less. But the love was never diminished. They would always have New York.

In 1989, Hubert was back living in New York City's Hell's Kitchen neighborhood. She was sipping on a margarita in her backyard one afternoon when her agent phoned about an audition for *The Fresh Prince*. She was to go to the Minskoff

Theatre at Forty-Third and Broadway in Times Square and wait for a fax with the character breakdown. She was excited, but the fax took so long to arrive that she fell asleep waiting for it. Later that day her agent called her with big news.

"They want to do a test," said her agent excitedly. They wanted to fly her out to Los Angeles to audition in person. However, the excitement soon faded.

"At the audition they gave me nothing," said Hubert. "They wanted a Denise Nicholas prototype, which I was not. They wanted a lighter-skinned woman."

She was convinced they didn't want her. Hubert had admired Nicholas for years but felt she was the furthest thing from her. When she sat down in the waiting room before the LA audition she closed her eyes and tried to gather her thoughts. Auditions can be nerve-racking experiences, wrought with pressure and disappointment. Actors universally loathe them. Most end in failure and the constant rejection can wreak havoc on a thespian's fragile ego.

Janet slowly breathed in and out. She had this. She would nail it whether they wanted her or not.

When she opened her eyes Denise Nicholas was sitting directly across from her. Nicholas, fairer than she, had guest-starred on sitcoms like *Benson*, *227*, *Diff'rent Strokes*, and *Amen*.

She was in awe of the green-eyed beauty. Hubert had known about her hardships. Nicholas alleged she was beaten in an Arizona motel in 1973 by her then-boyfriend, singer Bill Withers, after she told him she was leaving. Her sister was shot dead and left in a rental car at LaGuardia Airport in New York.

Hubert felt a kinship with every Black actress, an undying loyalty that every theater actress has toward her peers.

But she had dealt with her own struggles as well. They often related to her skin. Prized by gentleman callers, derided by casting directors. Sometimes in the same day. Often in the same day. Always in the same day. A pain she was forced to conceal. It's not funny when the mirror is your enemy.

You can't bring pain into an audition for a comedy show.

Hubert once auditioned for a role on *The Cosby Show* as a member of Clair Huxtable's book club. She nailed the audition. Cold. Her agent was told she did a great read and was "very pretty." But she was "just too dark."

Hubert was crestfallen. She vowed she would never again allow anyone to wound her because of her complexion. She would embrace all that she was. More fervently than ever in the past. The nerves had dissipated by the time she entered the *Fresh Prince* audition room in front of about thirty others. There was no pressure to be felt; she was convinced she wasn't getting it.

"I didn't even try," remembered Hubert.

She pulled her dark hair back into a dancer's bun and began to read with a casting director playing Philip Banks. She didn't exactly bowl the room over with her lines.

It was an okay read.

Denise Nicholas probably did better.

In the name of authenticity, Quincy Jones even suggested

that a bourgeois Black guy like Uncle Phil would more likely than not have a fair-skinned wife. But the Borowitzes insisted on going with Hubert because they felt she was the best actor for the part.

It's what she did in between the words that did it. The body language. The looks. The head tilts. The reactions. The side-eyes. It couldn't be taught.

But it wasn't Aunt Viv, and it wasn't acting.

It was Janet.

"It was Black girl attitude with elegance," said Hubert.

The Black girl from Chicago won the role.

"Ooohhh! You're British! Solid!"

His mother called him "Fraimy," after Elfraim, his middle name.

Shortly after World War II, Britain offered an invitation to those living in any territory of the British Empire to come to the United Kingdom to help with post-Blitzkreig reconstruction. Construction workers, masons, carpenters, anyone with useful skills to rebuild the country was welcome.

When Joseph Marcell was eight his father moved the family to London to put his carpentry skills to good use, thinking it would provide a better future for his family. The Marcells settled in Peckham, a small village of run-down houses and social and economic problems to match. Unemployment, muggings, and property damage were the fabric of everyday life in South London. Crime ran rampant and racism cut a path across London.

A commonly seen sign hanging in store windows read NO DOGS, NO COLOREDS, NO IRISH.

But the family settled in as well as could be expected. Marcell began his schooling, made friends, and rarely seemed to cause mischief.

Caribbean culture often dictates that children are expected to exceed their parents' station in life, to gain more skills and education than the previous generation received. Joseph's father enrolled him in a technical school, thinking electrical engineering would be his path ahead.

Marcell thrived, achieving a Higher National Diploma in electrical engineering—the equivalent of completing two years at university in the United States. He began practical industrial training (think internship) in 1968 at the first water-cooled reactor in Britain, two hours away in Southampton.

On the weekends he would return home to hang out with his friends. Evening excursions often included tankards of ale and attempts to win over pretty South London girls, if one could muster the confidence.

On one such trip night, while walking across Waterloo Station into London and back toward Peckham, he and a group of friends passed by the Aldwych Theatre, home to the Royal Shakespeare Company.

"My friends and I noticed outside the theater there were these huge, enormous billboards with Black actors, entertainers, and singers," said Marcell in 2020. "We had never seen anything like this before."

With no prior interest in the theater, they decided on the spot that they had to see what was inside. For a half crown, two shillings, and sixpence, they sat in the farthest row and watched the American Negro Theatre as part of the World Theatre Season festival.

It set Marcell's mind on fire.

"From that point on, each weekend before we went out to commit our sins we went to the theater," said Marcell. "It just stuck with me."

The son of a St. Lucian carpenter decided he wanted to be an actor.

His father, the man who had worked with his hands his entire life, did not take the news well. His mother, however, proved a fine mediator and it was decided that Marcell would move to South Hampstead, a hub for drama students and home to many theaters. He quickly enrolled in Hampstead Studios, a small acting school. His first gigs upon graduating in 1970 were in children's theater, with the goal of joining the actors' union.

Only somewhat comfortable with the living he had carved out, he continued to keep his ear to the ground for better opportunities. He got word that the Royal Shakespeare Company was looking for nonwhite actors and auditioned for a spot in the coveted theater company in January 1972. His speech from *Julius Caesar* won him a spot, and armed with that and his Shakespearean background, Broadway soon opened its doors as well. He grabbed a role in *Sherlock Holmes* and seized the chance to dabble in shows around the country, from New York to Los Angeles, San Francisco, and Oakland on the West Coast.

Marcell worked out a few small parts in British television but he didn't harbor Hollywood dreams like most actors. He had been trained in the English tradition. Shakespeare was his language. The stage was his home.

"Wait, This Isn't in the Script!"

Originally, NBC wanted Ron Glass to play the role of Geoffrey the Butler. Who? Exactly. He was one of the detectives on *Barney Miller*. When one producer suggested Glass there was a groundswell of support behind him. But Glass wasn't English. He was an American actor doing an English accent.

Another producer had seen Marcell in the Royal Shakespeare Company. That could work because Borowitz wanted him to be British. For some excellent reason.

In 1990, he was performing in the first London production of the August Wilson play *Joe Turner's Gone Away*, about an African American boardinghouse in Pittsburgh in 1911. His agent informed him that there was interest from NBC in Los Angeles about a sitcom pilot that was being developed. The producers sent Marcell a script and asked him to record his audition on VHS and send it back. After they gave him some notes he sent another tape. This time they asked if he could immediately come to Los Angeles.

Upon arrival Marcell was picked up at Los Angeles International Airport and taken to a hotel in North Hollywood to rest. The next day he was ferried to NBC in Burbank, which he knew from *Rowan & Martin's Laugh-In*, a popular American sketch comedy show in Britain in the late 1970s. There he went through a series of meetings where he met Will Smith, Brandon Tartikoff, Quincy Jones, and Debbie Allen, who would direct the pilot.

During a break in meetings he went outside to smoke. An enormously sizable man with thunderous steps and a laid-back, agreeable disposition had the same idea. He sauntered over in a way that only a leviathan could.

"Hey, how you doin', man?" said the giant.

"I'm quite fine, thank you," replied Marcell.

"Ooohhh! You're British! Solid!" replied the man.

"Nice to meet you. I've only just flown in. I'm Joseph Marcell."

"Whoa, man! I'm James Avery."

They quickly bonded over their love of Shakespeare and the theater. Avery positively beamed when he told Marcell about his year at the London Academy of Music and Dramatic Art. He also informed Marcell that he had just performed South African playwright Athol Fugard's *Sizwe Banzi Is Dead*.

(Though they could not know it then, their friendship would last twenty-five years.)

Back upstairs the producers wanted Marcell to read with Smith in the flesh. Their hilariously comedic contrast was evident before they were even given scripts.

They began the first scene from the pilot. Smith threw Marcell, the serious British stage actor, for a loop when he began to ad-lib fast and furious. Marcell had never had any experience with this sort of improvisation. He had always relied on structure. The words on the page had always been infallible. This approach had never failed him.

But here his instincts and training did just that.

Smith sensed the discomfort and stepped it up even more. He wrapped Marcell in a huge hug, picking the actor up off his feet and carrying him around.

"Wait, this isn't in the script! Have there been rewrites?"

"Nah, man, I just throwing some stuff in there," laughed Will. "Just go with it!"

A disciplined actor, sure. But he *was* an actor. He knew how to go left when he was supposed go right. Even if he had only gone in a straight line his whole life.

This was exciting and silly and fanciful and fun.

The audition was a smash.

"You funny as hell, man!" cheered Will. He told the producers they had found Geoffrey. Quincy smacked the table. Tartikoff offered no opposition.

(In his 2021 biography, *Will*, Smith writes that his demand that Marcell be hired was his first power move as an actor.)

Another perfectly imperfect fit secured.

"People would say we got so lucky with the cast but it wasn't luck, it was racism," explained Susan Borowitz. "There just weren't many great roles for Black actors at the time. There had not been an explosion of Black shows yet. And there was so much talent, so we were able to cast great actors for every part."

Showtime

The show that would never happen needed an intro to match its insurgent energy. This would be Smith's go at the reins of leadership on the show and would become his calling card.

Will wrote and recorded those now-ubiquitous lyrics over Jazzy Jeff's bouncy track in under ninety minutes. The next day he burst into Andy Borowitz's office.

"The smile on his face was as wide as I've ever seen it," recalled Borowitz. Smith was just happy to be making music again, and they both knew this track had met its mark. The producer, a novice to hip-hop but no fool, either, quickly gave his emphatic endorsement. But they still needed the visuals.

The iconic sequence where Smith catches a cab to the

Banks house on fictional 805 St. Cloud Road in Bel-Air—"Yo, Holmes, smell you later!"—was shot by a second-unit crew a week after NBC picked up the show for thirteen episodes. Smith had achieved his primary objective since moving to Los Angeles—landing a job—and he carried the celebratory energy to match. Everything was starting to feel real.

It was Will's idea to hire the director of his "Parents Just Don't Understand" video and keep the same charming cartoon aesthetic. They even hired the guy who played Will's cranky, overbearing mom in the original.

"It was magical," said producer Mara Lopez, who oversaw the shoot.

The first episode cleverly picks up from the moment the opening credit sequence ends.

Will arrives to the Bankses' cavernous mansion and is met by their unflappable, staid English butler, Geoffrey. It's a prompt introduction to the rigid demarcation between the wealthy and the servile that is necessary for a household like this one to function.

"Tradition dictates that I shall address you as Master William," says Geoffrey.

"How about," counters Will, "His Royal Freshness? Ah, that's dope!"

Uncle Phil and his wife, Vivian, then greet Will in the family room. Aunt Viv, a strong-willed nurturer, is quick to embrace him while Uncle Phil eyes Will with skepticism and is tripped up by their culture clash.

"The plane ride was stupid," says Will.

"Excuse me?" replies Uncle Phil with consternation.

"Nah, I'm sayin' the plane was dope."

"EXCUSE ME!!"

"I had never seen anybody with the charisma like Will," said Borowitz. "He was killing it. He was so in command of his performance it was otherworldly. Watching it as a producer, it was astounding."

NBC president Brandon Tartikoff chuckled offstage in agreement.

Within moments of meeting his cousin Carlton, clad in plaid shorts with a pink cardigan draped over his shoulder, Will begins to land jabs at every available opening. He settles on two quick, easy targets: Carlton's height and nonexistent sense of Blackness.

In the second act Carlton admires Will's first tuxedo, a gift from the Bankses, which he'll wear to a party Uncle Phil is throwing for members of his law firm later that night.

"Wait till we come downstairs in those tuxes," says Carlton. "People might not think we're twins but I bet they'll think we're brothers."

"I don't think you have to worry about anybody mistaking you for a brother," jabs Will.

After being roundly dismissed and viewed with distrust as he delivers one well-timed barb after another, the relationship of the show's characters quickly falls into place.

But Will is not without support. The Bankses' youngest daughter, eleven-year-old Ashley, tired of being babied and overprotected, embraces him without condition. She is the only member of the family who doesn't judge Will or make assumptions. He reciprocates her trust by treating Ashley like a peer and showering her with encouragement and attention.

Tatyana Ali nervously fidgeted in her chair offstage while makeup artist Joann Kozloff applied the finishing touches to the girl's makeup. Tatyana's mother stood sentinel, trying to calm her down and get her to focus on her lines.

The stage manager called for Ashley before one final brush-down of her jet-black hair. She took her mark and steeled herself before striding onto the set. In this scene that was Will's bedroom, where he had just stapled a poster of Malcolm X to the wall.

A softer side of Will emerges from behind his comedic wrecking ball. He empathizes with Ashley's plight. She wants to express herself. So he teaches her to rap. She hates the clarinet, so he gives her drum lessons. She's sick of ballet, so he lays out the finer points of hip-hop dance.

"The audience is falling for Will," said Parsons. "You can see it happening in real time."

"I Know Where I Come From"

The last scene—which would ultimately decide the show's fate—sees Will saunter into the Bankses' family room to join Uncle Phil's stuffy party, where well-heeled friends are waited on hand and foot as Phil frets about whether neighbor Ronald Reagan will show.

Will rocks purple-on-white Air Jordan Grape 5s with no laces, his fluorescent yellow hat cocked to the side and his cummerbund absurdly pulled up around his chest. Uncle Phil is mortified.

No member of this high-society menagerie is spared Will's darts. From Uncle Phil's law partners to do-gooder socialites, it's open season. After the party Will and Uncle Phil clash for the first time in what will become a staple of *The Fresh Prince*.

Uncle Phil introduces the partners in his law firm.

"These are my partners in the law firm of Firth, Wynn and Meyer," says Philip.

Will: "Hey, Earth, Wind and Fire."

(The tiny burst of wordplay got one of the shows biggest laughs.)

The incensed patriarch admonishes Will for his "flippant shenanigans."

"Everybody is talking about changing me into something I don't want to be," says a frustrated Will. "I'm a joker, I play around, I have fun."

"That's the problem," says Uncle Phil. "You can't take anything seriously."

"You have the problem," retorts Will in the first of his many acts of rebellion. "Somewhere between Princeton or the office you got soft. I remind you of who you are and what you used to be. You forgot where you came from."

"I know where I come from," says Uncle Phil, his baritone dropping an octave. "I encountered bigotry you couldn't imagine. Now you have a nice poster of Malcolm X on your wall, but I heard the brother speak!"

Will is taken aback, his defiance receding, the impression he had of Uncle Phil now radically changed.

"You actually heard Malcolm speak?" he asks with deference.

"That's right. So before you criticize someone you find out what he's all about."

Will tries to plead his case but is shut down by his uncle.

"I know what you're all about," says Uncle Phil just moments after chastising Will for doing the same to him. "I'll deal with you in the morning."

The uncle heads off to bed. The nephew sits down at the piano. He pulls the bench close and lowers his head. He begins to play Beethoven's "Für Elise" just as he did the first time Borowitz met him in Quincy Jones's living room.

The audience, emotionally spent, delivers a rousing ovation.

The cast members return to the set to soak up the adulation and wrap each other with hugs when the director Debbie Allen calls cut.

"When I saw Will at the piano at Quincy's house I knew that was the end of the pilot," said Borowitz. "I wasn't sure how to get there but I knew I had my ending."

"The piano scene is what grounded the relationship," added Susan. "Uncle Phil saw enough of Will's raw potential to really think there was something there. They both earned a little respect for each other so that the relationship could develop into caring."

"*The Fresh Prince* was a classic fish-out-of-water story," Andy continued. "The network wanted it as broad as possible, so I thought this was a way to puncture all that."

It played true to Quincy's push for duality. More importantly, the interaction between Uncle Phil and Will had shone through in a way it hadn't in rehearsal. Execs and writers alike were giddy with thoughts of potential story lines and themes that could revolve around the pair.

Producers were amazed at how Avery shared the stage with Will and stood up to his charisma. How he held his ground without detracting from Will or compromising his own performance.

"He had to have a tremendous amount of power," said producer Ilene Chaiken. "He was the anchor. He's what grounded the show."

The audience buzzed as they filed out. Borowitz breathed a sigh of relief before heading to the wrap party.

"I just didn't want to be the white guy who fucked this up trying to do the white liberal version of the show," he recalled.

An hour later Smith and Borowitz, star and creator, stood in the patio garden of the Beverly Wilshire hotel, sipping spirits and recapping the show while wondering if it had a future. Will loved the immediacy of the response from the crowd. It felt like he was onstage with a mike in his hand— something he had secretly been longing for.

For a moment their cautious optimism seemed to give way to a strange new joy. A seed was planted. A family was born.

It worked.

"Heaven has to be like a cross between a Sir Mix-A-Lot video and Roscoe's Chicken 'N Waffles"

Coming off the pilot, NBC and Tartikoff got very excited and set up Smith for a busier-than-usual press blitz in the two months leading up to the September 10 series premiere. The press conferences, photo shoots, and promos were piled on thick. Tartikoff began to feel all tingly, telling anyone who would listen that he thought *The Fresh Prince of Bel-Air* could have the biggest NBC debut since 1985's *The Golden Girls*. NBC dreamed of capturing 30 percent of the viewing audience, which made ad agencies very giddy.

When Tartikoff wasn't trumpeting Smith's virtues he was whispering quiet encouragement on set to his newest star. People noticed how personally Tartikoff invested himself in both the show and his young protégé.

Smith reciprocated the sentiment. At an early NBC press party, in which Smith donned a velour sweat suit and large gold herringbone necklace with a diamond studded *Fresh Prince* pendant, he stepped to the microphone to say a few words about Tartikoff. A lighthearted freestyle spilled out.

"Carol Burnett, she was right in swing / And you hit it

on the head with that show called *Wings*," said Smith with a grin, much to the delight of the president.

Later during a break in the action, Tartikoff walked over to Will and put his hand on his shoulder. He thought Will's charm and self-confidence could carry the lagging network back to prominence. But he also carried concern for the young talent—he knew there was so much to come.

"I hope you know who your friends are, Will," he said. "Because this coming year you're going to have a lot more people wanting to be your friends than you could ever imagine."

Tartikoff had gone from skeptic to lead cheerleader. He might not have known hip-hop, but he knew what transcendence looked like on the screen.

"He'll bring the world of hip-hop to white audiences," spouted Tartikoff, "and be a star like Eddie Murphy."

Tartikoff was an avowed Murphy fan, so this was the highest praise. Eddie had been credited with bringing African American cool to white audiences and making Black swagger more digestible for those who were unfamiliar with it. When Tartikoff hosted *Saturday Night Live* in 1983—the only network executive ever to do so—he appeared in a sketch as an exaggerated version of himself. As an executive dressed in a black leather suit, gold chains hanging over his bare chest, and an over-the-top swagger, he tried to pitch Murphy absurd show ideas.

Murphy enters the executive's office wearing the exact same suit, as if he just stepped off a comedy stage.

"Eddie, my man," says Tartikoff. "What it is?! Listen, a couple of my main men at NBC have put together some sketches that are positively bad."

"Why do you want me to look at sketches that are terrible?" asks Eddie.

"No, I mean bad like good."

"Oh, you're talking Negro."

"We want to team you up with Jimmie 'JJ' Walker. We're gonna call the show *Ebony & Ebony*."

"I'm not interested."

"All right, we're gonna give you a Saturday morning cartoon show about you and your family called *The Murphs*. But they're not blue, they're Black. I can make you bigger than Gary Coleman."

"I got parts on my body bigger than Gary Coleman."

(Ironically, Murphy created his own family cartoon called *The PJs* nearly twenty years later.)

But the point of the sketch worked—white people being so comfortable with Black mannerisms and speech thanks to Murphy that they clumsily tried to adopt them. Murphy's charisma and likability greatly contributed to the phenomenon and Tartikoff was a big believer that Smith's *Fresh Prince* would have a similar impact.

The *Los Angeles Times*' Daniel Cerone described Smith two months before *The Fresh Prince* aired:

He's network television's first embodiment of a fresh generation. He's a prime time tap into the urban street market, which is pumping rap music, loud new fashions and an Afrocentric political consciousness into mainstream society faster than the booming bass tracks of a def jam.

But all the praise just made Will nervous. All the little things, the ones he'd never expected (or known to expect, given his lack of experience on camera), began to wear on his confidence. He was constantly being told not to look at the camera—the exact opposite of an impression-making rapper's instincts.

"People are expecting a lot, and I've never done any acting, so I don't want to be compared to anyone," he told the *Times*. "I have a natural feel but let me practice first so I can be proud of what I do. This is really new for me."

It didn't stop NBC executives from freely tossing around names like Murphy, Michael J. Fox, and Oprah.

"[Tartikoff]'s making me nervous, comparing me to Eddie Murphy and stuff like that," said Smith. "Slow down a little bit. Man, let me practice first. My head is still spinning a little bit."

The pilot hadn't even aired and he was already expected to get from behind Eddie Murphy's shadow, the biggest Black movie star in the world.

In *Will*, his 2021 autobiography, Smith says:

I found my thing. The world of acting unleashed all the artistic impulses within me. It was the first external canvas that felt big enough to hold the landscape of my imagination. My musical expression always felt normal and constrained by the limits of my skills and talents. Making music felt like being in a great neighborhood, whereas acting felt like being set free in an infinite universe. . . . Acting encompasses all things that I am—storyteller, performer, comedian, musician, teacher.

All he had to do now was do it.

6

A Fresh Start

Season One taped at Sunset Gower Studios on Melrose. Generally, Karyn Parsons, Janet Huber, and whatever female guest star was there for the week would arrive first for hair and makeup, usually around 6 a.m. The men and young Tatyana Ali arrived later since they didn't require as much assistance. At least not from the show's staff—at some point each week Will would make his own arrangements to get his hair cut for each show.

It took him a few years to achieve that TV-perfect fade and lineup, but he would sometimes shell out hundreds looking for the right barber along the way. A Philly man couldn't leave town, let alone go on his own national TV show, without a tight fade.

"Of course," said Smith, "we invented the fade."

The cast would normally receive their scripts via courier over the weekend, generally focused only on the scenes in which they appeared. They spent the prep time forming ideas about how they would deliver their lines once they came to work.

On Monday morning there would be a table read with the cast, crew, writers, and directors. Everyone ran through the script a first time, as a group, without any direction or notes. This gave them the chance to feel out which jokes worked and which didn't. These early table reads were also bonding sessions in which the actors could get to know one another without the pressure of having to deliver the perfect line or nail a scene in front of a live studio audience.

"I met Will at the first table read," said Parsons. "He was this kid with big cute floppy hands and feet with energy. He always had this happy-to-be-here vibe."

The first thing Will said to Parsons was "Isn't this great?!"

The first table read of the first season was particularly energetic thanks to optimism and anticipation about what this team could accomplish together.

"Will and Alfonso were chasing each other around the table," said Ali. "Their energy was so great."

They hit it off so fast. They all did. A big reason was food. The original Roscoe's Chicken 'N Waffles, one block north, became the cast's favorite spot. By 1 p.m. or so most of the gang would pile in James Avery's Jeep Grand Cherokee and head over for lunch. Unsurprisingly, Avery could put away large quantities of the famous fare, often going for a half chicken smothered with gravy, two waffles, a side order of red beans and rice, with a helping of corn bread.

Roscoe's became a bit of a running joke on set. In Season Three, Episode 10, "Asses to Ashes," it even got a shout-out when Will described his ideal heaven. "To me heaven has to be like a cross between a Sir Mix-A-Lot video and Roscoe's Chicken 'N Waffles," says Will. "See, it's like I can have a leg in one hand and a breast in the other."

One downside, however, was the mass food coma that would overtake the cast afterward. Requests would fly to do rehearsal while sitting down in the living room. Eventually things got so bad the producers began to debate whether or not it was worth their time and professional capital to ban midday Roscoe's trips.

But sometimes if the script needed a lot of work, the producers would come downstairs and tell everyone to go home for the day. Most were off in time to tune in at 8 p.m. on Monday nights to watch the show when it aired. In the early days Will would pop a tape in the VHS to record it so he could watch his performance over and over like an athlete studying game film. The writers, meanwhile, would be up all night punching up the script.

Tuesdays' revised scripts would normally be in better shape, and the cast would begin the day rehearsing and figuring out what blocking (how the actors moved around set and in relation to one another) felt the most natural. They would work through the nuts and bolts until both cast and directors were all comfortable with it. Writers would come in toward the end of the day to sit around the studio and watch it like a play.

Afterward the entire group would sit down in the family room and go over what they had just done. It was an environment where everyone felt like they could speak up and toss out suggestions for jokes and various lines. The writers were all the while scribbling furiously on their legal pads.

The script was usually locked in by Thursday morning, though changes could technically be made right up until taping. The actors would arrive to get into hair, makeup, and wardrobe for a dry run of the episode—a rehearsal in front of an empty studio to work out the unexpected kinks that don't pop up until all the pieces are in motion. Cameras would roll during this to check that the imagined blocking and pacing between dialogue beats made sense for film.

Fridays, shooting days, *game days*, were electric. Audiences began to file in around 6 p.m. The tickets were always free. There was usually a comedian to warm up the audience (in later years it would be D. L. Hughley on the mike). If his act didn't match the week's audience's vibe, he would tailor it accordingly. Warm-up isn't about the person talking; it's about the show to come next. Crowd work—interacting with audience members off the cuff—usually did the trick and put everyone in a good mood.

Breaks in the pretape flow were filled by Jazzy Jeff on the turntables, scratching and spinning down the clock to showtime. When Will got out of his dressing room—first on set, always—a mini DJ Jazzy Jeff and The Fresh Prince show would break out. At first this was just a little treat for the audience, a free hip-hop concert to accompany your free (well, they were all free—it was broadcast TV) *Fresh Prince* episode. Later, as the show became a hit, tape day became an event. A place to be seen and heard. The wings of the studio started to fill with actors from other shows who had the night off, models, athletes, and beautiful aspiring starlets.

"It was like a club," said Smith. "It was the place to be. Everyone wanted to be at a *Fresh Prince* taping. We just wanted it to be like a party. We wanted everyone to have a good time. It was just like what me and Jeff started out doing."

When it was time for the full acting cast to be introduced, they would each emerge from their dressing rooms banging instruments to the DJ's beat—drums, bongos, tambourines, anything that could liven up the crowd. The idea was to work the crowd into a frenzy so they would be ready to laugh and have a good time.

The cameras would finally start rolling at 8 p.m. The actors would take their marks. The clapperboard would snap. And then it was on.

Will and Carlton Explain the (Black) World

Despite how nerdy, geekish, awkward, and . . . itchy Carlton is portrayed by Alfonso Ribeiro on camera, the character is always *way* more confident and self-assured than Will. It's the thing Carlton has that Will most wants. Recognition of that envy, that unspoken admiration, hangs in the air above their relationship at all times. It is the driving factor in Will's protectiveness of Carlton, and it shows in how he treats Carlton when others are around. As the series progresses we notice that Will's verbal jabs at Carlton are fueled by his desire for attention from others, not just to belittle his cousin.

Will and Carlton's relationship is the comedy core of

the show. But it also serves as a vehicle to touch on some early serious themes. It was the main vehicle for producers as they deftly navigated the balance between comedic fun and the show's important messaging on the Black American experience, without becoming too preachy or too heavy for white audiences to handle. All this with a nearly all-white writing staff that had little knowledge of virtually any aspect of Black culture.

Carlton has no fear of the world, whether through naiveté or the protection of privilege, while Will's guard is up at all times. We're left to presume that the confidence-versus-insecurity dynamic stems from the two characters' socioeconomic backgrounds, but it's also clearly influenced by the roles of their fathers.

Will and Carlton's ability to puncture the veneer of their respective safe realities is what makes *The Fresh Prince* different from any Black sitcom that preceded it.

The two most popular Black sitcoms that preceded *The Fresh Prince*, *The Cosby Show* and *A Different World*, rarely put the characters in contact with other African Americans who hadn't shared their own lived experience. And certainly not under the same roof. (In fact, Cosby didn't want a hip-hop ethos anywhere near his show.) Like the Cosbys, the Banks family had largely been insulated from aspects of urban culture until Will arrived. It shed a light on a slice of Black culture they had never got to experience, whether they were ready for it or not.

Will and Carlton's opposing Blackness, which pulls one

toward the other, was always at the core of their relationship and the show's comedy.

"Will and Carlton saw Blackness differently but I think there was more overlap than not," said Andy, who admits he knew little about Black culture.

He continued: "A lot of it came down to style. Will was coming out of hip-hop culture, which was considered the default cool culture. If you were cool and you were hip that's what you were into. But he could play Beethoven and he was also very bookish in a sly way."

Here's Susan:

"I was about as white suburban as they came. I just thought, I am not qualified to write this. It really petrified me. There were a couple Black kids at my school but I wouldn't say I was friendly with them. You tend to stay with who you are. They're not gonna be your closest friendships. Unlike what Disney shows try to tell you, that there's always the one Black best friend. I don't think that really happens in reality."

"Homeboy, Sweet Homeboy" (Season One, Episode 5) guest-starred a then-unknown Don Cheadle as Will's best friend, Ice Tray from Philly. According to Susan, Cheadle was dating Karyn Parsons at the time, but won the role after blowing away the producers with his audition (Parsons and Cheadle had met on a Coke commercial months before she was cast). Cheadle's Tray and Will are two peas in a pod here. This is the life that represents safety and familiarity to Will, though Tray is even more cavalier about his studies.

Carlton's response? "You poor disadvantaged inner-city youth."

Back in Philly, Will had tried to hide his curiosity and seriousness about schoolwork. Tray represents what Will is holding on to about Philly, even though he knows it's holding him back. It is our first look at Will's personal conflict: his unbending loyalty to his past and his desire to grow as a person.

But here's the subtextual wrinkle—not only does Will feel like the Bankses won't let him be himself but in several ways his friends from Philly won't either, based on their expectation of what they think he should be. Will goes along for fear of being labeled "soft." Or worse, a sellout. An irreversible kiss of death in the Black community.

He's hid his bookish leanings for fear of being branded a sellout, the very same thing he now accuses Carlton of being.

He batters Carlton ceaselessly for supposedly conforming to a life he didn't want, despite secretly envying his privileged cousin's freedom all along.

No one in Carlton's Bel-Air life would chastise him for being his true self. Except Will, as a bandage to conceal the wounds on his own fragile ego.

This conflict mirrored Will Smith himself. The Fresh Prince, the real one back in Philadelphia, is a character created by a high school kid to gain acceptance and to shield himself from loneliness, fear, and his greatest shame—cowardice.

Will Smith, the character, pretends to be the Fresh Prince to mask his insecurities and vulnerability.

It was new territory for how a young African American male was portrayed on prime-time network television. His often confused, resilient, hardheaded, complex self railed against anything he perceived as threatening. Against anything that made him less than authentic. Even if his version of authenticity was inherently flawed.

But the end result was that he would also be the most loyal defender of his "weird cousin," the same cousin he would come to realize would show him love like no other. Who would help him—force him to—process the damage he'd been holding inside all along.

Yet they would still disagree about what was the *right kind* of Black (neither understanding that there is no such thing).

Carlton's and Will's definitions of Black success are drawn from their fathers. Will's is absence, and defined wholly from the outside. His father had walked out on him twelve years prior to when the show begins. He feels success when he feels closest to the peers of his Philadelphia upbringing. Carlton's is defined by his father, whom he had watched operate as part of the establishment—wealthy, high achieving, elite, and able to seamlessly assimilate. Carlton had never been questioned about this vision of Blackness until Will moved in.

In an act break in the pilot, Will looks in the mirror and is horrified because he's dressed in Carlton's argyle sweater, with its pinks and greens. But when Carlton looks in the mirror he sees the best version of himself. While the show would explore the meaning of Blackness to much more dramatic effect in upcoming seasons, here the producers were working to preview that discussion while establishing the show as a comedy first and foremost.

In the first episode devoted entirely to the duality (there's Quincy's word) of Will and Carlton's dynamic, their tug-of-war over Blackness, Will bets Carlton he wouldn't last a day in the hood. In "72 Hours" (Season One, Episode 23), penned by Rob Edwards, Will drops Carlton off at DJ Jazzy Jeff's crib in a run-down building near MacArthur Park, the once-picturesque oasis on the corner of Wilshire and Alvarado in Los Angeles that has become overrun by crime and homelessness. Carlton has been challenged to spend two days inside the world he perceived Will to have come from.

(Yes, the title "72 Hours" doesn't correspond with the final script—it had been whittled down in rewrites and nobody noticed to change it.)

When Will returns to Jazz's run-down (except for a very real black-and-white head shot of Karyn Parsons, pasted to the wall and assumed here to be the object of Jazz's affection, Hilary) apartment days later, he finds Carlton dressed in baggy clothes, a gold chain, and a do-rag. In a stamp of approval, Jazz's crew has given him the nickname C-Note. Carlton sees Will enter, jumps up off the couch, and delivers a resounding "Yo, whassup!"

"Carlton, you look like a pirate," says a confused Will.

"Stop fronting! You know this gear is chill!"

"Why you talking like that?"

"Yo, how you playing me, Prince? Yo, you *dissin'* me!"

The live audience gasps and howls with laughter as they see Carlton in a strange, uncomfortable new light. But it's funny as hell. Carlton has proved something by seamlessly fitting in with Jazz's crew in his own way—a strange mash-up of an over-the-top hood and his practical, analytical self. He makes hip-hop flash cards to quickly learn the language.

"Yo, C-Note," the gargantuan six-foot-five, three-hundred-pound Tiny Lister, who most famously played Deebo in the 1995 film *Friday,* asks with deference. "How do I figure my net worth?"

"Ayo, how many times I gotta tell you? Write your questions down and I'll hook you up later."

"I'm sorry, that was rude of me."

With that, Carlton has put Will in the corner for the first time in the series.

"We actually wanted to write the episode for Alfonso, not Carlton," said Edwards. "Alf is cool; he's got swagger. He's an amazing dancer and singer. He's a star. But he's a star who can play a really good goofball."

Ribeiro lit up at the first table read for "72 Hours."

"I've been waiting to do this!" he exclaimed, fist pumping in the air.

Carlton's huge statement to Will is that he could be cool in the way Will chooses to be cool. That *his* way of moving through life is a choice, just as Will's has been, too.

Off camera, Will, the real one, could be nerdy in a very appealing way. When he wasn't the life of the party he could be

very withdrawn. His introspective and academic self would leak through the cracks. He would get lost in his thoughts and wonder about his own self-worth or manhood. But in public he always wanted to please.

In this way, Carlton, the B-player, arguably became the Fresh Prince's most important character for opening America's eyes to different slices of the Black experience. Beyond that, he also planted seeds of the eventual merger of nerd culture with hip-hop culture.

African American scholars, writers, creators, and activists have long pushed back on the idea that Black people are a largely distorted, homogeneous blob of exact experiences and interchangeable parts, thoughts, and feelings. That there is an easily identifiable sameness to be viewed through a singular lens. That each Black person's experience is indistinguishable from the next.

Of course, those backgrounds and life experiences vary as much as those of any group and the ambitions of Black folk are an ever-evolving kaleidoscope. But it could have once been reasonably argued that some Black people's own narrow self-perception due to external forces, lack of ambition, or a fear of that communal self-inflicted ridicule for "acting white"—thus selling out—has played a significant role in furthering stereotypes from the amusing to the destructive.

Not smiling in photographs. Valuing unrelenting masculinity over a broader emotional spectrum when there's room for more. Sexual conquest as proof of manhood. Little interest in "white" extracurricular pursuits. Resistance to ex-

panding one's horizons in music or culture or thought. And the biggest offense of all—being ashamed to take pride in academics, a mindset that has contributed to the creation of a permanent Black American underclass.

From the *Washington Post*'s Clinton Yates in 2012, nearly fifteen years after *The Fresh Prince*'s end:

> Nerd culture has hit a cultural high point. More than ever, people are going out of their way to self-identify as "nerdy" as kind of an ironic way to put an affable twist on parts of their personalities that they might otherwise be ashamed of. . . . The rise of the black nerd is upon us. Unite!

Since then, as Millennials and Gen Zers steeped in *The Fresh Prince* from their most formative years have taken control, the irony and stigma Carlton battled on the show have all but vanished. Black nerd culture, as varied and polylithic as broader Black culture, is becoming the rule rather than the exception.

Skinny jeans, Vans, vintage 1980s style—the evolution of nerd chic—dominate urban streetwear and have become the preferred style in both fashion circles and high school hallways.

Donald Glover's critically acclaimed *Atlanta*, Jordan Peele and Keegan-Michael Key's *Key & Peele*, Issa Rae's *Awkward Black Girl* empire, and even our forty-fourth president have had more in common with the Carlton end of things than Will Smith's conception of "cool" captured in the show back then.

"The best thing about Obama is that he's a Black nerd," Glover shares in a 2013 stand-up act, "because I'm a Black nerd and that shit was illegal until like 2003."

One afternoon on set, this very subject came up. Borowitz asked Will why he thought Carlton was cool.

Will: "He's cool to his friends, which is all that matters. You just have to adjust your gauge for what cool is."

Then just twenty-one years old, Will and his generosity as an actor surprised Borowitz. He didn't go to the writers and insist Carlton be as much of a joke as possible in order to get laughs at his expense.

In fact, it was just the opposite.

Will was the fish out of water.

Carlton was the fisherman who threw him back.

• • •

From his days writing on the wholesome family sitcom *Full House*, Edwards would usually write the last five minutes of the episode, which quite often contained the sweet, feel-good lesson in which the characters learn something about themselves, grow a bit, and leave the audience satisfied.

All three of our Season One themes dovetail splendidly: Blackness, comedy, and the cousins' ever-strengthening bond.

"This is my time to gloat," says Carlton. "I won the bet. I humiliated you in front of your peers. You said I couldn't handle Compton and I did. You're just embarrassed that I beat you at your own game. You always act like I don't measure up to some rule of Blackness that you carry around."

"Hold up!" Will counters. "You don't judge me? You do everything but carry around a big old gavel. You treat me like I'm some kind of idiot because I talk different."

Carlton pauses. "Differently."

"You did not win the bet. Our bet was that you couldn't spend the weekend in Compton and you didn't."

"That's only because you came and got me," replies Carlton.

"If I hadn't come and gotten you, you woulda got yourself killed."

"Oh?" counters Carlton. "And why was that important to you?"

"Pffft! It wasn't!"

"Admit it, Will. You like me. You like having me around."

"Aye, Carlton, take it back, man."

"Face it, you love me."

"My brother! You wanna take this outside?!"

"What's on the Menu?"

In the late 1980s and early '90s it was just commonplace for Black-themed shows with all-Black casts to have white showrunners. *The Cosby Show, Roc, Martin, Parenthood.* But none of those were based in hip-hop or starred a streetwise rapper.

The writing staff is the backbone of every show. But with this rather experimental program, led by two producers who admitted they weren't exactly HBCU grads, the task of blending the right amount of hip-hop with broad comedy chops was more critical than ever.

One of the first people the Borowitzes called was veteran writer Rob Edwards, an African American Detroit native in his late twenties who set the tone. His father was a doctor and he himself had been a private school kid, but Rob still knew his way around the hood.

"I kind of understood both sides of the premise," Edwards told me. He took the meeting dressed in chinos and a golf shirt, made Andy and Susan laugh, and got offered the job in the room. They certainly liked that he was a veteran of *In Living Color* and *A Different World*, the latter of which had become the highest-rated Black sitcom on television the year before.

"This wasn't *Family Matters*," said Edwards. "With a show like that they're just basically writing white families. You had to get deeper into the culture. Andy and Susan were very open about what they didn't know."

Forty-four-year-old Samm-Art Williams, the elder statesman of the writers' room, was a burly six-foot, eight-inch mountain of a man with a gruff but sweet disposition despite the fact that he called everybody "nigga." He was an OG actor and playwright from deep down in Burgaw, North Carolina (population 1,476), but had moved to New York in 1973 to chase the theater. There he caught on with the Negro Ensemble Company, Douglas Turner Ward's ensemble that claimed Debbie Allen, John Amos, Laurence Fishburne, and Denzel Washington among its alums.

And then there were the (white) comedy writing room regulars:

Shannon Gaughan had been plucked by Borowitz from Keenan Ivory Wayans's new sketch show *In Living Color*, after an unsteady start there. "Keenan was wonderful and intelligent," she told me, "but I was rather intimidated by what they were doing. I didn't know enough about that aspect of Black culture and just felt I wouldn't be good at it." (Gaughan had gotten the job anyway, but old friend Andy promised he'd built a room ready to teach over at *The Fresh Prince*.)

Another *Color* vet, Sandy Frank, had also come from the basement of the *Harvard Lampoon*, just like Andy. Frank's crowning glory had been *In Living Color*'s infamous "Men on Film" recurring sketch with Damon Wayans and David Alan Grier. Rounding out the staff were Cheryl Gard (*A Different World*) and the quirky southern writer Lisa Rosenthal, who was known for turning scripts around with lightning speed.

The wild card was someone with no experience at all. Will brought childhood friend Bennie Richburg with him from Philly to check him and make sure he stayed authentic to the culture. Richburg's title on set was Homeboy Philly Consultant (no joke, check the credits).

"Will and his guy Bennie would go back to Philly on hiatus weeks and bring back all the new slang and give it to the writers," recalled Susan. "So it prevented the show from looking like it was written by a bunch of creaky old white people. Even though Andy or I weren't creaky or old at that point."

It didn't take long for the culture clash to make itself known. How about the second week? In "Bang the Drum, Ashley" (Season One, Episode 2) written by Gaughan, the character Jazz makes his first appearance. Right away he starts to drop digs on Uncle Phil in the same way Will would.

The chorus of Black writers threw up a blinding red light.

"No damn way someone is going to go into a Black household and start cracking on a real Black father with no pushback," said Williams, who was immediately backed by Edwards. "Especially if they're not family!"

Andy thought the jokes were hilarious.

"We did it all the time on *Family Ties*," said Susan.

"But you couldn't do that in a Black man's house," Edwards said, explaining that upsetting the home would be a sign of disrespect.

"Let's just try it," Sandy Frank offered.

"Hell, naw," snorted Williams. "If that stays in I'm quitting."

Edwards said he'd follow him out the door.

They needed to find a creative solution. The writers had to figure out how to keep the jokes, make them authentic and funny. They kicked ideas back and forth.

"Why don't they just throw Jazz out of the house?" Edwards offered.

The room exploded in laughter. The jokes stayed in and one of the show's longest-running gags was born.

In this first case, Uncle Phil commences the toss after he learns Jazz has agreed to cover for one of Will's get-rich-quick schemes (he pawned Ashley's violin) by teaching her how to play the drums instead.

(The idea is based on writer Gaughan, who had been driven insane when her ten-year-old son took up the drums after two uninspired years of piano.)

Andy thought it would be great to toss him out of the actual *Fresh Prince* house. One problem: the real Bel-Air mansion, at 251 North Bristol Avenue, was 11.8 miles away from the studio where the show was taped. That exterior of the house was only used for establishing shots. So a small crew made the trip over to the exterior, laid down a safety mat, and had Jazz run out of the house and jump onto the mat nearly fifty times. Problem was, Jeff Townes was not a stuntman and had to get a crash course in how to kinda land properly. By the end his back ached and his elbows and knees were covered in bruises.

"We ended up getting this great thing from a cultural difference," laughed Edwards.

In "Not with My Pig, You Don't" (Season One, Episode 4), Uncle Phil's mother (Virginia Capers) and father (Gilbert Lewis) fly to Bel-Air from Philip's humble birthplace of Yamacraw, North Carolina (two seasons later a production mistake would turn that into Yamacraw, South Carolina), for the weekend:

"What's for dinner, Granny?" asks Will.

"Oh child, turkey, stuffing, cranberry sauce," responds Granny.

"That's not a Black Thanksgiving," said Richburg. "We don't eat pumpkin pie. We eat sweet potato pie."

Since Richburg was there to keep it accurate and authentic, he pulled Borowitz aside. If the script wasn't changed, he said, Black people would know it was written by a white person. That menu was just all wrong.

"Gimme ten minutes."

He came back with a list that included sweet potato pie, collard greens, ham hocks, macaroni and cheese, and yams.

After an on-the-spot rewrite, Geoffrey Butler, who's off to the store, hesitantly reads Richburg's list back to Will's southern granny in his distinguished, weary English accent.

"One pound of lard, four handfuls poke greens, and a big ol' slab of fatback."

"Now if it comes to more than a dollar they're cheatin' you," advises Granny.

The audience lost it.

"The explosion that went off in the audience was indescribable," remembered Andy. "It just felt really rich, satisfying, and real."

"Bennie Richburg was the exclamation to every sentence in the writers' room," said Susan. "When Will brought him in we all just fell in love with him."

From that point forward the Borowitzes began to take on less of an active writer's role and became more facilitators and curators of the cast's and writers' ideas.

"I didn't always get it right but I listened intently. It was such a kind of dangerous mission for me to try to pull this off as a white guy because the audience was in a position to be the most critical and aware of the mistakes we could make," Andy said.

It all paid off. At the end of the first season *The Fresh Prince* won an NAACP Image Award.

"To get that type of appreciation from the Black audience was so meaningful to me," said Borowitz. "To this day it's still one of the most moving nights of my career."

"Dipping Them in Chocolate"

The show was building up serious steam and the Will and Carlton Comedy Train was barreling along.

Despite their adversarial, competitive coexistence, Will and his cousin come to depend on one another immensely. Their selflessness and devotion to each other, which would be crafted over several seasons and ultimately define their relationship, is glimpsed early in the show's run.

In "Chubba Hubba" (Season One, Episode 3), also penned by Rob Edwards, Will has an eye for Mimi Mumford, the hottest thing at Bel-Air Country Club.

This is the first of many examples where either Will or Carlton would set aside one of their differences in service of one another.

"It's kind of like an inverse '72 Hours,'" notes Edwards.

Growing up in Detroit, Edwards went to nearly all-white Cranbrook prep school, twenty-two miles northwest of the city, in Bloomfield Hills, and on which Bel-Air Academy is based. Utah senator and former Republican nominee for president of the United States Mitt Romney is an alumnus.

Edwards would take the bus home to Detroit but by the time he got off he'd be dressed in "appropriate gear" to hang in the hood.

"There's a phenomenon where all affluent Black people code-switch," he explained. "We talk differently if we're at a barbecue than we do if we're at a ball. It all depends on who's around."

"In the writers' room all of the writers would constantly be talking about inside Black stuff, you know. Things that only Black people know. We had some of our best, funniest ideas come from those conversations."

One of the producers once heard an executive describe the show as wanting it to be like some kind of *The Brady Bunch*. Some network executive wanted the Black version of the popular suburban 1970s sitcom.

"We call that dipping them in chocolate to get the Black version," said Edwards.

Of course the writers and Borowitz weren't about to go that route—they all might have quit—but Edwards *did* know of a particular *Brady Bunch* episode that he wanted to adapt in a *Fresh Prince* way. *Brady*'s "Two Petes in a Pod" episode sees middle son Peter run himself into the ground trying to juggle two dates who are unaware of the other's existence. Was there a more perfect idea for aspiring Romeo Will?

In *The Fresh Prince*'s version, Will essentially transforms into his alter ego Kip Smithers, a (slightly cooler) carbon copy of his cousin Carlton, to win over actress Victoria Rowell's Mumford, a beautiful Black woman Will spots at a country club. Rowell, who would go on to star in *Dumb and Dumber* the following year, beat out twenty other actors for the role,

playing daughter to tough-as-nails thoracic surgeon Dr. No
(Richard Roundtree).

After getting a crash course from Carlton on how to be a
gentleman—a hilarious send-up of Audrey Hepburn's Eliza
Doolittle in *My Fair Lady*—Will is decked out in plaid shorts
and a rainbow pastel sweater slung over his shoulders as he
enters the dining room. Will soon finds out that Mumford—
who prefers to go by Mimi—really wants a criminal bad boy
"from the streets. I'm tired of whitewashed preppies."

Will bangs a U-turn at 100 miles per hour and accelerates
past his true self as an outlandish convict cartoon character
to win her over. Soon he's running back and forth like Peter
Brady when Dr. No enters the room, and so changes perso-
nas on a dime.

It was a terribly difficult task for such an inexperienced
actor to pull off, but the live studio audience was left in hys-
terics as Will put his all into trying. Even when he tripped up
mid-bit, they laughed.

"Sorry, Mom," Will said to his mother, Caroline, between
takes, who was in the audience. "I messed up!"

In the final act Will comes in with dark sunglasses, a
bowler hat, and a pimp limp circa 1940s Detroit. He quickly
explains the plan to Carlton before approaching Mimi.

"Now remember, I'm wanted in five states," says Will.
"I'm hiding out from the police for robbin' a gun store. And
what did I do before then?"

"You went to Penn State," replies Carlton.

"I went to the state pen!"

"I thought Penn State was bad enough."

They approach Mimi.

"Allow me to introduce KIP," says Carlton. "That's his street name; it stands for Konceived In Prison."

"I thought you said you rowed crew?" asks a puzzled Mimi.

"Nah, nah, baby. I said I wrote for the 2 Live Crew."

Driving home, Will and Carlton's duality and love for each other is cool. But man was it fun just to get laughs.

However, there was at least one person who wasn't exactly laughing.

Will was also getting unsolicited opinions and criticism from Bill Cosby, who had nothing to do with *The Fresh Prince* and was busy shooting seven days a week on his own show, which taped in New York.

Cosby thought Will was soiling Black culture with his silly dances and Fly Girl impersonation. He completely despised the hip-hop ethos and felt Will's antics were setting back the course of Black television progress he had set out with his *Cosby Show*. To Bill, Will Smith's act was sophomoric, and unbecoming from a young man who was now becoming one of the most prominent Black male role models in the country. When Cosby offered notes on how Uncle Phil and Aunt Viv should parent their children—tougher, with more discipline—Janet Hubert was incredulous.

"One day Bill Cosby called Will and told him he was helping to destroy Black culture," said Susan. "He was a real pain in the ass. He also did the same thing to Martin Lawrence.

Then he goes out and adds a street-smart hip-hop character on *The Cosby Show*. If you can't beat 'em, join 'em, I guess."

The (then) beloved actor had a long history of dishing harsh critiques of Black culture and values in everything from education, to speech patterns, marriage, and family. He had made similar calls to fellow comedians Richard Pryor, Eddie Murphy, and Keenan Ivory Wayans in the past, all of whom had begun to grow tired of Cosby's "godfather" act.

According to Eddie Murphy, Pryor once said, "Tell Bill I said 'have a Coke and a smile and shut the fuck up.'"

Will Smith had adored Cosby. He was a role model. Will had grown up watching *I Spy* and *Fat Albert* and listening to his famous comedy albums. And Cosby was from Philly, born just fourteen miles from Will.

So just the fact that Bill Cosby knew who he was meant a lot—but he'd do his own show the way he wanted to.

"Keep Your Hands
Where I Can See Them"

Mr. Smith not only can sing, write and dance,
he clearly can act too. . . . Mr. Smith displayed a
strong sense of comedic timing, mugged for the
camera at will, improvised dialogue with alacrity.
—*New York Times,* September 17, 1990

The Fresh Prince of Bel-Air had quickly established itself as one of the early hits of the fall prime-time network
TV schedule. The ratings were solid, its cast delivered
a steady stream of family-friendly laughs, and its young
star was capturing attention, including from the *New York
Times:*

It's pretty easy, and not just because I'm basically playing myself," Mr. Smith said of his switch from the concert stage to the soundstage. "With rapping, it's a lot of lines you have to learn anyway. And with a rap performance, I can't just call out for the script if I can't remember a line. If I forget a line, I'm lost. So this is a lot easier."

But now it was time for the show to test its legs a bit. A show built from Philadelphia street culture couldn't get by with ignoring the full story of all that meant. The struggles of life at the margins needed to be part of the show. Serious topical themes, taken from real life, had to play a role in any media about contemporary Black America, one way or another. What would be *The Fresh Prince*'s first swing at it?

The crew decided on racism in policing.

In "Mistaken Identity" (Season One, Episode 6), Will and Carlton are pulled over in an expensive Mercedes owned by Uncle Phil's law firm partner and accused of a string of auto thefts before being jailed with no evidence.

"Will and [writer] Bennie Richburg were telling me all these stories about being pulled over by cops in Will's Benz," said Borowitz. "Pretty much every Black man in the cast and crew had had a similar experience."

While growing up in Cleveland, Borowitz had never experienced this firsthand but he was keenly aware of discrimination and overt acts of racism toward African Americans in his hometown.

The Hough Riots of 1966 was the first such incident to shape his views on policing and race. The Hough neighborhood of Cleveland had a population of 66,000, of whom 90 percent were African Americans living in poverty. More than a fifth lived in dilapidated housing, nearly all owned by white absentee landlords. A failed urban housing renewal effort actually displaced more people than it housed. Half of the single mothers in Hough were teenagers who then themselves gave birth to a third of the population. The schools were segregated and poorly equipped, the welfare system spotty, trash pickup inconsistent, and street cleaning nonexistent.

But far and away the biggest problem was the boiling tension between the residents and the Cleveland Police Department, whose ranks were 93 percent white and carried a barbaric reputation for its abuse and disregard of the Black community.

In his 2003 book, *Ohio and Its People*, George W. Knepper writes, "The focus of Black anger was the police force, which had a reputation for crude racism and insensitivity towards the needs of law-abiding Blacks. Neglect and disregard had created frustration and desperation in the neighborhood."

From a July 1966 story in the *New York Times* titled "Hating Police Is a Way of Life in the Hough Area of Cleveland":

By day, the Negro section here is a sun-dappled, decaying slum filled with quiet people going about their business. By night, it is dotted with fires and filled

with armed patrols and jeering residents. . . . The Negroes of Hough hate the police and in many ways the
police hate the Negroes of Hough. The police appear
to be adding to the problem by being chronic under-
achievers in diplomacy.

In that July of 1966, at a popular white-owned diner
on the corner of Seventy-Ninth Street, called the Seventy-
Niner and frequented almost exclusively by Black people,
the owner put up a sign in the window that read NO WATER
FOR NIGGERS, which resulted in a small but rowdy mob forming in the parking lot. They launched rocks at the windows
in retaliation. Glass shattered. The owner retreated. The police arrived an hour later.

For the next five days a thousand residents and more
than 2,100 police traded bullets, rocks, bottles, and Molotov
cocktails.

Injuries, regret, and every imaginable form of hate flooded
the streets.

Four people were killed, fifty injured, and 275 arrested.

"The underlying causes of the riot," a review board
wrote, "are to be found in the social conditions that exist in
the ghetto areas of Cleveland."

Borowitz watched all of this from the safety of his living
room in quiet Shaker Heights, six miles and a world away.
Surely an eight-year-old white Jewish kid could not effectively process what he was seeing in the smoldering embers
of a faraway hellscape.

But he knew what he saw. For the ills of the world cannot be shielded from the eyes of knowing children.

Borowitz would become sharply aware of both social injustice and change almost preternaturally. He recalled when Cleveland elected its first Black mayor, Charlie Stokes, after the riots as "a proud day."

His script was heavily influenced by the stories of police interactions with Black folks who worked on *The Fresh Prince*.

The traffic stop in the third act of "Mistaken Identity" highlights how vastly different Will's and Carlton's views and experience with policing are. When they are stopped, Will knows the drill and accurately predicts each step of the interaction. Carlton is relieved to see the officers, knowing they'll be able to provide him directions.

They've been asked by Henry Firth, Phil's partner, to drive his Mercedes to Palm Springs to meet the Bankses and Firths for a weekend retreat while the elders arrive by helicopter.

But first, as always, the comedy must be established. Halfway to Palm Springs, Will asks Carlton to share his snack. Carlton agrees on the condition that Will carry himself as a perfect gentleman over the weekend. Will agrees.

"Good, what do you say to an Oreo?" asks Carlton.

"I say whassup, Carlton!" responds Will.

They soon get lost and pull off into a residential neighborhood and, while driving slowly trying to find a sign for the freeway, are pulled over. When a police car lights up and sounds its siren behind them Will instinctively flies into panic mode.

"Punch it, man, we in a Benz!" he says, alluding to the age-old practice of police targeting Black males in expensive cars.

"Are you crazy?" retorts Carlton. "I call this a lucky break. A policeman is our friend. We can ask him for directions."

"Listen to me. When he comes up keep your hands on the wheel," instructs Will.

When the officer steps to the driver's side door, Carlton cheerfully extends his hand to shake.

"Good evening, Officer. I'm Carlton Banks."

"Keep your hands on the wheel," the officer curtly replies.

It's already clear that Will and Carlton's experiences with policing have been thoroughly shaped by their respective upbringings. Will has spent a lifetime in the hood, dodging, running from, and being mistreated by Philadelphia's notoriously brutal police department. Carlton's privilege and wealth have shielded him from the same mistreatment his entire life.

Given his exceeding naiveté, it is entirely possible that this is his first experience with law enforcement.

"Where you headed?" asks the cop.

"Palm Springs! And where might you be headed on this fine evening?" Carlton cheerfully replies.

"Great, Carlton, now he's gonna want to see your license."

"Yeah, right."

"Lemme see your license," says the officer, played by longtime *Simpsons* voice actor Hank Azaria.

"Now, I have to warn you this picture was actually taken without contacts and the height is a typo. I'm actually a lot taller."

"Fool, this is not the *Love Connection*!" scolds Will.

Back at the station in the interrogation room, Will shrewdly gives Carlton the advice to keep his answers short and sweet. Instead he gives long, rambling, hardly believable answers about the fact he lives two doors down from the Reagans and that his parents just took a helicopter to Palm Springs.

The boys aren't read their rights, are questioned without a lawyer, and are thrown into a holding cell without any evidence. When Uncle Phil arrives he reads the hapless cops the riot act and threatens a lawsuit for violating so many of Will and Carlton's rights.

"Who the hell do you think you're talking to?" booms an irate Uncle Phil. "When you got this alleged confession out of them did they have a lawyer present? No. Because I'm their lawyer. Did you notify their parents? No. Because we're their parents. Just open the cell and let those boys out now or I'm gonna tie this place up in so much litigation your grandchildren are gonna need lawyers!"

The audience roars its approval.

While the focus of the episode is to highlight Will and Carlton's distinct life experiences, it is hardly lost on the viewer that mistreatment of Black motorists in general has plagued policing for generations.

It is not uncommon in African American households for elders to walk their children through each step of a traffic stop and emphasize the importance of being calm, respectful, and patient, and to obey lawful orders. And, as equally important, to even obey orders that are not lawful, under fear of death. Such a conversation likely never took place in the Banks household.

At its core the way policing is carried out toward African American motorists is about limiting mobility and the accompanying freedom it affords.

It is about control.

During slavery in the antebellum South, slaves were largely forbidden to ride horses. It was even frowned upon if a freed Black man were to be in the saddle. Not being able to ride a horse would make it nearly impossible to maintain a farm in the rural South, where most Blacks lived. In the 2012 Quentin Tarantino movie *Django Unchained*, the titular character, played by Jamie Foxx, is challenged when he is seen on horseback.

When Django and his ally Dr. King Schultz (played by Christoph Waltz) arrive at a large southern plantation the owner is aghast that a Black man is on a horse.

"It's against the law for niggas to ride horses in this territory," says owner Big Daddy, played by Don Johnson.

"This is my valet," replies Schultz. "My valet does not walk."

"I said niggas on horses—"

"His name is Django and he's a free man. He can ride what he pleases."

(Ironically, according to the Smithsonian Institution, one in four cowboys on the American frontier were Black.)

In the 2020 PBS documentary *Driving While Black*, filmmakers assert that the way African Americans are policed today, particularly when driving a car, bears a strikingly similar pattern of disregard, terror, and potential for violence that were hallmarks of the ruthless slave patrols, roving bands of armed men hired to police and monitor slaves in the antebellum South.

To instill fear, obedience, and terror. But most importantly, their objective was control. Of both movement and thought.

They are sworn in and given a mandate.

The 1854 North Carolina Slave Patrol Oath reads as follows:

I, _____, do swear, that I will as searcher for guns, swords, and other weapons among the slaves in my district, faithfully, and as privately as I can, discharge the trust reposed in me as the law directs, to the best of my power. So help me, God.

Here is the oath a police officer takes for the state of North Carolina Highway Patrol in the present day:

I, _____, do solemnly swear that I will be alert and vigilant to enforce the criminal laws of this State; that I will not be influenced in any matter on account of personal bias or prejudice; that I will faithfully and impartially execute the duties of my office as a law enforcement officer according to the best of my skill, abilities, and judgment; so help me, God.

They are virtually interchangeable.

Slave patrols would stop any Black man, free or otherwise, demand papers, question them at length, create false charges, imprison, and beat them excessively. They were instructed to carry out their duties in the most brutal, terroristic, and often as sadistic a manner as possible.

The threat of administering violence was to be ever present. The thought that slaves were chattel was never to be forgotten.

A slave patroller first had to convince himself that Black people were not human.

In a July 2020 article dissecting policing and race, the *Atlantic* wrote:

The problem lies in the organizational cultures of some police forces. In the forces with an us-versus-the-world siege mentality. In the ones with the we-strap-on-the-armor-and-fight culture, the ones who depersonalize the human beings out on the street. All cruelty begins with dehumanization—not seeing the face of the other, not seeing the whole humanity of the other. A cultural regime of dehumanization has been constructed in many police departments.

It's also true that over the course of American history, law enforcement has constantly been used to enforce racial hierarchy. Police brutality reflects the legacy of racial lynchings, and some of the habits of mind that are still embedded in American society and in its police departments.

This is why Will's instinctive reaction is fear. He tells Carlton to book it because in his learned experience, the only possible outcome is a bad one.

His next reaction is born out of the first—compliance. This is the least likely path to a beating, vague, superfluous charges, or his mother, Vy, making funeral arrangements.

Will almost immediately gets out of the car without being told, doesn't argue, and puts his hands on the hood and earnestly surrenders.

"The Open Road Less Traveled"

America marveled at the invention of Henry Ford's Model T car, a conveyance that would change the country perhaps more than any invention since Benjamin Franklin dared to dangle a key on a kite in a thunderstorm.

The horseless sleigh.

It made a rural country that much smaller and gave birth to the Industrial Revolution and America's dependency on oil.

At first built slowly by hand, cars could be built at a rate twenty times faster after the invention of Ford's assembly line. A new model every year with improvements and up-grades. Better handling, stability, and comfort. Previous owners clamored for a new model each year. By 1935 there were 15 million Model Ts operating in the United States, just in time for Roosevelt's New Deal, which saw the creation of the Works Progress Administration, which was the first major infrastructure project of its kind, building roads and bridges all across America.

The rate at which the Model T could now be built created a brand-new market: the used car.

Owning a car was no longer a luxury but instead was essential. It was now available to a much wider segment of America. Everyone wanted a part of that dream. African Americans were no exception, especially those in the South who flocked to northern cities to escape the searing insult of Jim Crow and daily threat of lynchings. The Great Migration of Blacks to the North, and better-paying jobs, gave birth to the Black middle class. Many Black folk could now afford automobiles.

By the 1950s the role of the car on the American landscape was transformed from mode of transportation to leisure. Ford and other manufacturers were advertising cars as a way to see the country, which gave rise to America's new obsession—the vacation. Automobile manufacturers would splash the pages of magazines with colorful ads showing happy families in picturesque locations far from workaday life, in pursuit of leisure and holiday.

To again handle the proliferation of new cars, President

Dwight D. Eisenhower signed into law the Federal-Aid Highway Act of 1956. The first phase was 41,000 miles of highway touching every state in the continental United States, called the National System of Interstate and Defense Highways. In other words, freeways.

"As the roadways open you have a parallel movement occurring," said Alvin Hall, host of the *Green Book Podcast*. "For white Americans they are discovering the joy of the open road. Maybe drive to California or see the Grand Canyon. For African Americans the open road is about seeking a better life."

But as with anything in Black life, the hope and optimism brought by the open road often led to indecision and fear and anxiety. Traveling could often be a danger for the Black motorist, whether from harassment at the hands of police or inadvertently wandering into towns or counties that were inhospitable to Black people. Whites-only signs were everywhere, often threateningly worded, since the Supreme Court made separate but equal the law of the land in 1896 in the landmark case *Plessy v. Ferguson*.

To aid Black motorists in finding safe haven while traveling America, a mailman from Harlem named Victor Hugo Green began publishing an annual guide listing businesses, restaurants, gas stations, repair shops, and towns that were welcoming to Black travelers, called *The Negro Motorist Green Book*. Since many hotels and restaurants did not serve Black customers, extensive pre-trip preparations had to be made. Oftentimes families would prepare enough food for several days for the trip, for fear of not being served. They would bring portable toilets or sleep in their cars or abandoned barns. Some folks would carry gallons of gas in the back of their station wagons, which in itself could be dangerous. Black children would stare out the windows of hot, stuffy cars and see white children happily playing in motel pools.

Other than Black skin, out-of-state licenses were a dead giveaway that Black motorists were in the wrong place. Making matters worse were unwritten local rules that would often change from one jurisdiction to another and could spark violence in one town while simply eliciting dirty looks in another.

One user of the *Green Book* was the late U.S. representative John Lewis, who served thirty-three years in Congress and was an ally of Dr. Martin Luther King Jr. As he recalled in Gavin Wright's 2013 book on civil rights and economics, *Sharing the Prize:*

> There would be no restaurant for us to stop at until we were well out of the South, so we took our restaurant right in the car with us. . . . Stopping for gas and to use the bathroom took careful planning. Uncle Otis had made this trip before, and he knew which places along the way offered "colored" bathrooms and which were better just to pass on by. Our map was marked and our route was planned that way, by the distances between service stations where it would be safe for us to stop.

The worst of all dangers could be "sundown" towns. These were places that all Black people had to leave by sundown or risk arrest, property damage, beatings, and even death. By law or will of the people, African Americans were prohibited to be within city limits of thousands of towns across America after dark.

The *Green Book* ceased publication in 1966 after the passage of the Civil Rights Act of 1964, which prohibited discrimination based on race, color, religion, sex, and nationality.

But African Americans' problems behind the wheel were just beginning.

"The Police Department as a 'collection agency'"

Still today the subject of driving while Black has exploded onto the national scene with a series of high-profile killings and the proliferation of cell phone cameras, which have captured shocking images of Black people—almost always young males—being pulled over for trivial infractions only to die in brutal fashion at the hands of police, often poorly trained and with racial biases and nefarious motivations, and who are often exonerated.

Beyond the threat of death are often financial implications that can cripple entire communities. Let's take a look at the U.S. Justice Department's 2015 investigation of the Ferguson, Missouri, police department in the months after unarmed teen Michael Brown was shot dead in the street.

The results are staggering.

First, for context, 67 percent of Ferguson's roughly 21,000 residents are Black while accounting for 76 percent of those arrested. About 93 percent of Ferguson's police officers are white (the same percentage as the Cleveland Police Department during the Hough Riots forty-eight years before).

African Americans made up 85 percent of vehicle stops and 90 percent of those ticketed during traffic stops. Further, 93 percent of all people arrested in Ferguson were Black. Of traffic citations issued by police based on less objective methods—usually officer observation—80 percent went to Black motorists.

A staggering 96 percent of people arrested because of an outstanding warrant during traffic stops were African American. This is largely due to police taking advantage of the fact that many Black drivers—not just in Ferguson—do not possess a clear understanding of many processes of the legal system. A common belief is that failing to pay a ticket can result in arrest. (It cannot.) So, many avoid traffic court dates. But failing to show up at traffic court will result in a judge issuing a bench warrant for your arrest (complete with additional fines). This can lead to missed time at work and possibly job loss for many who struggle to even pay the amount of the initial ticket. Skipping court is actually the preferred outcome from the perspective of the Ferguson Police Department and the city manager (who processes and manages all incoming fines) because now they are obligated to make arrests and collect even more money.

As a result of so many people skipping court, the most eye-popping finding of the Justice Department's investigation is revealed. In 2013, despite a population of around 21,000, the city's municipal court issued 32,975 warrants for arrest. That breaks down to about ninety warrants a day. The majority were for traffic offenses. Black males were overwhelmingly on the receiving end of these warrants.

This is a level of control that slave patrols could never conceive. Because slaves had no money.

"What we saw was that the Ferguson Police Department in conjunction with the municipality saw traffic stops, arrests, and tickets as revenue generators as opposed to serving," said President Barack Obama upon the report's release. He added that the Ferguson police were "systematically biased, placing minorities under its care into an oppressive and abusive situation," according to ABC News.

Then–attorney general Eric Holder echoed Obama, saying the Ferguson Police Department was acting as no more than a "collection agency."

(Coincidentally, sociologist, history professor, and civil rights leader James W. Loewen named Ferguson a "second generation sundown town" in 2014, given the way African American motorists were policed by its nearly all-white police force.)

For African Americans, the traffic stop can be a terrifying ordeal because of both the disproportionate use of force against them and the financial and legal implications, which can often last years.

The traffic stop is the entry point into the system.

Alfred Edgar Smith's poem "Through the Windshield" is emblematic of the hope that African Americans feel when embarking on a new adventure that often turns to pain and grief and disillusionment, and opens Gretchen Sorin's 2020 book *Driving While Black: African American Travel and the Road to Civil Rights*.

At the beginning of "Mistaken Identity," Will is grinning ear to ear after Mr. Firth agrees to his suggestion that he and Carlton drive the Benz to Palm Springs. There will be adventure, mischief, and of course bikini-clad women.

There will inevitably be disappointment.

But there is always a hope.

"When Was the Last Time You Smoked Weed?"

In October 2021, Philadelphia's city council approved groundbreaking legislation that will prevent police officers from pulling over motorists for low-level offenses like broken taillights and improperly placed registration stickers. The city's police department, like many others across America, had come under fire for targeting Black motorists.

The Driving Equality Law, approved 14–2, was the first of its kind in a major American city and expected to reduce the number of traffic stops by about 300,000 per year. Pretextual stops, when an officer pulls a driver over for a mundane reason in order to investigate a more serious crime, check for warrants, or conduct a search with no previous probable cause, are at the core of the driving-while-Black experience.

In the high-profile cases of motorists Sandra Bland in Texas, Walter Scott in South Carolina, and Philando Castile and Daunte Wright in Minnesota, all died after pretextual stops. Wright was pulled over for an expired registration sticker and an air freshener hanging from his rearview mirror.

In 2019, in Phoenix, Arizona, a La Paz County sheriff pulled over twenty-two-year-old Black man Phillip Colbert, again for an air freshener. The officer asked Colbert if he had any cocaine or heroin and tried to get consent to search his car. He asked Colbert eight times if he smokes marijuana.

(With the Driving Equality Law, Will and Carlton would have been spared a great deal of grief and headache, as their traffic stop would have been illegal.)

According to the Defender Association of Philadelphia, which represents 70 percent of those arrested in Philly for free, 97 percent of police vehicle stops are for low-level violations. Black drivers make up 72 percent of the stops while representing just 43 percent of the city's population.

"They Only See One Thing"

In the last scene of the episode, Will and Carlton find themselves in the living room of their Bel-Air mansion, as they often do. Will is frustrated by yet another negative interaction with police, and Carlton is struggling to get a handle on the moment.

"The police were only doing their job," says Carlton, trying more to convince himself than Will.

Will is irate.

"Those cops were just tryna do their jobs?!" replies an indignant Will.

"Don't get all bent out of shape."

"Man, you didn't learn nothing this weekend, did you?"

"I most certainly did," Carlton counters. "Always bring a map. If we would have had a map we wouldn't have had to drive two miles an hour and we wouldn't have been stopped."

"Oh," says Will. "So we were breaking the slowness limit. Well, I never heard of that law. But I did hear of this other law that's called 'If you see a Black guy driving anything other than a burned-out Pinto you better stop him because he stole it' law."

Will has had enough and turns to leave. Carlton digs in.

"What's your complaint? We were detained for a few hours and released. The system worked."

"Well, you're gonna be seeing a whole lot of that system. You just don't get it. No map is gonna save you. Neither is your glee club or who your father is. Because when you're driving in an expensive car in a fancy neighborhood none of that matters, because they only see one thing."

Will uses the back of his hand to tap Carlton's cheek, indicating his Black skin is the reason for the stop, before leaving him with his confusion and heading upstairs to sort through his own familiar frustrations.

A moment later, in the final scene, before going to bed

Carlton is still trying to make sense of what has transpired. As always, he looks to the most comforting figure in his life—his father.

"It was awfully nice for Mr. Firth to help us out," says Carlton. "I'll have to send him a thank-you letter."

"It shouldn't have happened in the first place, son," replies his father.

Uncle Phil heads to bed.

"Dad," the son calls out looking for safe harbor. "If you were a policeman and you saw a car going two miles an hour, wouldn't you stop it?"

Uncle Phil pauses, searches, and easily finds a moment from his vast life experience.

"I asked myself the very same question the first time I was stopped."

Uncle Phil turns to leave and Carlton sits dumbfounded and lost on the couch.

The camera pulls back.

"I would have stopped it," he says softly and without conviction.

A part of his world has been stripped away. Will is no longer a simple jester, but rather someone who has breached and reshaped Carlton's impenetrable worldview. That his father agrees with Will only serves to disconcert.

For the first time in the series an episode ends with no music or audience applause.

Only silence.

"Andy and Susan Have Left the Building"

By the end of the first season *The Fresh Prince* was the highest-rated new sitcom of the fall season—seventeenth overall—with a 12.9 percent rating, even outpacing fledgling *Seinfeld* in weekly viewers while the show about nothing was still struggling to finds its audience in its second season. *The Fresh Prince* was nestled safely in its 8 p.m. Monday primetime slot, ending each week just before America would switch over to ABC's *Monday Night Football*.

CBS was the Peacock Network's biggest competitor and would throw the kitchen sink at *The Fresh Prince* but without much success. There was *Evening Shade*, starring Burt

Reynolds, and *Uncle Buck*, based on the John Candy film and canceled after the 1990–91 season.

In December 1990, NBC happily filled a full twenty-two-episode order by adding nine spring episodes to the original fall order of thirteen. The network turned the Halloween episode into a two-part, hour-long show. They were so thrilled they took the unusual step of tacking on two additional shows at the end of the season to bring the total to twenty-five.

Since the Thanksgiving-themed episode "Talking Turkey" (Season One, Episode 12) incident, where the show's Black writers and actors stepped up to give the show authenticity and believability, Andy Borowitz had taken on less of a writerly role in favor of helping to nurture his staff's young voices.

"We had dispatched all opposition and by the end it was starting to feel like a fully cooked meal," said Borowitz.

At the end of the season, he was exhausted and almost completely burned out—it had been his ninth consecutive season of prime-time sitcom writing and producing.

But the event that sealed his decision was when Brandon Tartikoff dropped a bombshell that reverberated throughout Hollywood. He announced he would be leaving NBC in May 1991 to run movie studio Paramount Pictures. Borowitz was blindsided and felt abandoned.

He knew Tartikoff's pain and turbulence well. On New Year's Day several months earlier, the executive had been in a violent life-shattering car accident in which he and his eight-year-old daughter, Calla, were badly injured, according to a January 3 *Los Angeles Times* report. Turning on to U.S. Highway 50 near his vacation home in Lake Tahoe, his car was broadsided by another motorist, shattering his pelvis and several ribs. Calla suffered serious head injuries and was hospitalized for months but would eventually recover. Tartikoff would deal with both his own intensely painful rehabilitation and the guilt of putting his daughter in harm's way. (He was found to be partially responsible for the accident.)

Tartikoff was Borowitz's biggest champion and often shielded *The Fresh Prince* from network meddling. And now he was gone.

"He was the guardian angel," said Andy. "Now I would be in a situation where I could no longer lean on him.

"Brandon was one of the most competitive people I've ever met," he said. "He was so focused on NBC being number one. He was just ultrafocused on his legacy."

Tartikoff had guided NBC to sixty-eight consecutive weeks at the top of the ratings. He would obsess over his track record every waking moment. He loved the creativity and spontaneity of comedy, the chess match of building a schedule.

Tartikoff had fashioned himself into a celebrity executive who prided himself on being a daring ideas man.

"He had a huge ego but was willing to admit he was wrong if it ultimately meant he'd be more successful," explained Andy. "He was really good about recognizing other people's good ideas and allowing you room to work."

His competitiveness could get the best of him. He drove the team underneath him exceptionally hard and as a result could dole out his unique brand of disrespect, causing a certain dysfunction among his charges. But it was usually in controlled bursts in private. If a subpar idea was pitched, Borowitz would often call ahead to litigate with Tartikoff to minimize the impact crater on his subordinate's ego. More often than not, Tartikoff would acquiesce. But not without insult.

"He was pretty good at letting people know he was the alpha," said Borowitz.

Once, after viewing a unanimously cheesy promo for *The Fresh Prince*, Tartikoff unholstered his weapon. The spot saw Will Smith walking down Rodeo Drive in Beverly Hills.

"I'm here in Beverly Hills where the streets are paved with gold," says Smith before bending down and picking up a gold brick. "See, look what I found!"

Borowitz felt the cringe-inducing promo had to go, which Tartikoff cosigned before adding: "There's a reason this [promo] guy's not running an ad agency on Madison Avenue."

But mostly Tartikoff championed Borowitz and the young showrunner even found a degree of joy in these conspiratorial moments. It proved he was a trusted member of Tartikoff's inner circle, that they were making fun of the network together.

But that was over now.

"When you're starting a show and discovering what it is, that for me is the most creative part. Casting the show and getting it up on its feet and doing all those funny episodes was a great creative experience. I was dealing with tons of anxiety about whether we could keep it as good and what my role would be. As a show goes on the showrunner has much less creative leverage as the cast become more popular and more powerful. The writers were the voice of the show and we cultivated some great voices. They could tell stories I never could. I felt I should leave it in their hands. I realized after all these years I wasn't cut out to be in a writing room pitching and gang writing and working in a group. I had to ask myself if my continued involvement was going to make the show better.

"When I look at how it all came together . . . it all just happened," he continued before pausing. "I can't take credit for it."

There was also the real matter of Smith's growing power loosening the Borowitzes' creative control over the show. When the other actors would finish for the day they would go home. Almost always Will would head upstairs to the writers' room and bounce ideas, lines, and concepts off the writers. His influence and input on the show exceeded any other actor's by midseason.

He was intensely driven, wanted to earn his success, and one could see that he would soon likely have control over the operation. To some the show was just a job. But Smith lived and breathed it.

"We could see the handwriting on the wall," said Susan flatly.

As importantly, the job was straining their relationship at home, well, because they were constantly taking the show home with them.

"One of the hardest things about being a husband-and-wife writing team is that you can't go home from work," Susan explained. "We brought the work home. We didn't get enough of a relief. You just can't get away from work. We ate, drank, and breathed it. And as a result we were always at work. That was the worst part about it. I think it's a good thing for people not to work together."

Susan gathered her thoughts and continued: "You have a job, and it beats you up that day. You come home to your wife and tell her about it. Then she tells you about her day. That's normal. But we couldn't get away from it. It took a toll."

Sometimes around nine o'clock, when they were putting their daughter Alexandra to bed, the network would call. Then they'd be right back in work mode until midnight. As a respite they tried to find weekend activities like brunches or recitals or children's tea parties.

They often would hang out with their best friends, *The Fresh Prince* writer Shannon Gaughan and *Martin* creator John Bowman. But the topic would invariably come back to work. (Andy and Bowman once drove across country in Borowitz's father's Buick.) The rest of their friends in Los Angeles were writers they had met at Harvard.

"It was constant, constant, constantly work," she said with a sigh. "There was very little relief."

When there was a creative disagreement, the person

who felt the strongest usually prevailed. Normally, though, Susan would defer to her husband because he had run shows before.

Eventually they would make a rule that they were only allowed to talk about work on the car ride home. That lasted a week. The show was taking over their lives in a way they knew they could not keep up for very long. They started to plan an exit—they had been so smitten by their experience working with Don Cheadle as Will's friend from Philly in "Homeboy, Sweet Homeboy" (Season One, Episode 5) that they wrote and sold a pilot for him to NBC. Cheadle played a well-educated young man who returns to Detroit to work in the community, with the plan to run it in the time slot after *The Fresh Prince.*

"He was amazingly brilliant in that he could do both comedy and drama equally well," said Susan.

When the Borowitzes' resignation became official, in May 1991, one of Tartikoff's last official acts was green-lighting the Cheadle project before heading over to run Paramount.

"You guys are on the air," he told them.

Warren Littlefield, Tartikoff's presumed successor, loved the show as well, comparing it to "the best of Norman Lear."

But a week after Tartikoff departed, Littlefield killed the show. Resentments between the two had built up over years, and Susan thought he saw this as a way to get back at him—a knife to his final decision in the captain's chair and a final parting shot at Borowitz, one of Tartikoff's closest collaborators.

"Just a pissing war because Brandon did not treat him terribly well," said Susan. "Just a lot of pettiness. But it's probably the best thing that's ever happened to Don."

The Borowitzes determined they could not trust Littlefield. They thought he could reject all of their new scripts with a flyswatter all the way to San Bernardino out of spite. (The 8:30 slot would eventually go to Mayim Bialik's *Blossom* for the next four years, a duo NBC would dub the Fresh Prince/Blossom Hour.) Littlefield had no time for the Borowitzes' other creative pursuits, but he did still want them around to consult on *The Fresh Prince*, given the potentially volatile combination of Smith's growing power, Hubert's ever-expanding list of grievances, and a relatively inexperienced new showrunner.

They drew a line in the sand. They would only consult on *The Fresh Prince* if the new show was picked up. It backfired. Littlefield was unmoved and the show was shelved. Their agent instructed them to make nice, considering they were under contract for two more years and Littlefield wasn't going anywhere.

Borowitz retreated to the house he shared with Susan on Beloit Avenue, which backed up to Veterans Park in the Brentwood section of Los Angeles.

There, exhausted but hopeful, the boy from Shaker Heights, who used to make 8mm monster movies and sing a cappella, would relinquish all responsibility in favor of self-preservation and new creative adventures.

After a week of agonizing self-reflection, he had made his decision.

He was done.

Andy Borowitz had left the building.

Brandon's Epilogue

Brandon Tartikoff's time at Paramount was as rocky as it was short-lived. He was under tremendous pressure to duplicate his massive NBC success and pull Paramount out of the doldrums just as he had the Peacock eleven years before.

In 1974, at age of twenty-five, he had been diagnosed with Hodgkin's lymphoma. After six years in remission the illness returned shortly after he became the president of NBC Entertainment. He would sometimes attend chemotherapy sessions and meetings in the same day.

He died at UCLA Medical Center in Los Angeles on August 27, 1997, from complications from treatment for Hodgkin's disease.

Said his longtime colleague NBC executive Dick Ebersol, "At the last great moment when network television was a communal experience for America, Brandon was the one in charge of delivering the programs that created that experience."

He was forty-eight.

A Brief History of the
Black Family Sitcom

It is virtually impossible to tell the story of Black people on prime-time network television without starting with Norman Milton Lear. Born in New Haven, Connecticut, in 1922, the son of Herman, a traveling salesman, and Jeannette, a homemaker, he formed a close bond with his father by sitting in the family room, on their red leather chair, listening to fights from Madison Square Garden on the radio. That ended when his father was sent to jail for selling fake bonds and other fraud charges.

After high school and during World War II, Lear joined the United States Army as a gunner in the 772nd Bombardment Squad. After flying fifty-two missions in three years he returned stateside. Inspired by his uncle, he drove across country to Los Angeles to become a publicist. On his first night in Los Angeles he took in a play and sat behind Charlie Chaplin, whose son was in it.

To make ends meet he teamed up with his cousin Ed Simmons selling furniture door-to-door. It was Simmons's desire to become a comedy writer and he encouraged Lear to help him develop TV and movie ideas. Through a stroke of good fortune they were hired by Jerry Lewis and Dean Martin to write sketches, then became head writers of the popular NBC variety show *Rowan & Martin's Laugh-In*.

In 1959, Lear had created his first show, *The Deputy*, a half-hour western starring Henry Fonda. He wrote the 1967 film *Divorce American Style* with Dick Van Dyke and unsuccessfully tried to sell two television pilots. His third pilot, titled *All in the Family*, was picked up by CBS.

Lear became a television giant who once had nine shows on the air at the same time. His were the first shows to tackle abortion, menopause, and opposition to the Vietnam War. *The Jeffersons* featured the first interracial couple and kiss. One of his shows had the sound of a flushing toilet—considered in poor taste at the time—and debuted at 8 p.m., in prime time. Lear would retell the story a thousand times.

Lear earned an early reputation for creating shows with sharp, biting wit that weren't afraid to take on political and social topics of the day, and sometimes deliberately, in ways uncomfortable audiences weren't used to. Lear and Bud Yorkin, who hired Andy Borowitz fresh out of Harvard, first developed *All in the Family* in 1971. It starred Carroll O'Connor as a narrow-minded, cranky, homophobic, bigoted patriarch in blue-collar Astoria, Queens. *All in the Family* dealt with touchy, topical story lines that included race, religion, feminism, and antisemitism, often in unfiltered, highly offensive ways.

The characters Archie and his wife, Edith, were inspired by his parents. While the in-your-face overt racism Bunker spews wouldn't fly today, heck, not even twenty years ago, the intention of Lear's *All in the Family* wasn't to offend but to check the dimwittedness of racism and the failure of those who espouse such views. While making it funny, of course.

It worked. By its second season it began a five-year streak at No. 1 in the Nielsen ratings. Bunker, the deeply flawed, epithet-spewing curmudgeon struggling to come to terms with the changing world, is regarded as one of the best television characters of all time.

"The coons are coming!" laments Bunker when Black families start to move in the neighborhood.

"This is only the beginning but I think it's wonderful," chimes his liberal, feminist daughter, Gloria, played by Sally Struthers.

"Wonderful?" exclaims Archie. "We'll see how wonderful it is when the watermelon rinds come flying out the window!

"Archie Bunker ain't never gonna break bread with no jungle bunny!"

Interracial marriage, African American coworkers, diversity, and Black culture in general were all annoyances to Bunker.

Much as Will was an opposing force to the Bankses' wealth, privilege, and comfort, *All in the Family* needed an equally incompatible annoyance to puncture Bunker's racist worldview and force him to examine himself.

Enter his Black next-door neighbor George Jefferson (Sherman Hemsley). As irascible, grating, and equally unwavering as his counterpart, Bunker was chafed by his success and upward mobility but glimpses of fondness and humility would leak through the subterfuge. Lear used the men's wives to soften the mutual hostility of their bombastic relationship. Edith (Jean Stapleton) and Weezy (Isabel Sanford) often found themselves in a dizzying, exhausting juggling act to curtail their husbands' animosity.

Neither woman's values remotely mirrored her husband's. Yet they remained ever loyal. Because that's what women and housewives of the 1970s did.

In the last episode, their tearful good-bye is the show's most touching moment.

"Louise, did I ever tell you I love you?" says a remorseful Edith, as if to apologize for her husband's years of prejudice.

"Every minute we spent together," replies Louise.

At its peak *All in the Family* had an audience of 50 million, meaning nearly one in four people in America watched the show. And George and Weezy were a hit, so Lear began developing the idea for a spin-off even before the show ended.

The Jeffersons debuted on January 18, 1975, and early reviews weren't kind. From the *Hollywood Reporter:*

> *The Jeffersons*, a contrived show full of forced humor where everybody yells at everyone else in a totally unrealistic way—yet I have the feeling the show will work in spite of itself.
>
> If you look through all of the mistakes that were made in this episode such as exaggerated direction and writing people like cartoon characters, you see that somewhere there are believable people and a real situation. Hopefully someone will fix it.

The Jeffersons were the second nuclear Black family on television (*Good Times* had debuted a year earlier) and Lear had developed both shows. This was also the first-ever look at Blacks who had acquired wealth. George ran a chain of successful cleaning stores and they left Bunker's Hauser Street in Queens for a luxury twelfth-floor apartment on the Upper East Side of Manhattan and hired a maid.

The Jeffersons would ultimately run for eleven seasons and 253 episodes, making it the longest-running Black sitcom, only recently surpassed by *Tyler Perry's House of Payne.*

"There Ain't Never Been a Better Woman Than That!"

Maude, played by Bea Arthur, was the polar opposite of O'Connor's Bunker in every way. A liberal feminist, Maude strongly pushed Democratic ideology.

Of particular concern was the well-being and progress of minorities and the underserved. She was a strong believer in civil rights and racial equality, and highly offended by any notion to the contrary.

Of course *Maude* itself wasn't a Black sitcom by any definition, but it did introduce audiences to two of the most memorable Black sitcom mainstays ever—Florida and James Evans. Played by Esther Rolle and John Amos, Florida and James (he was introduced as Henry on *Maude*) were two of the earliest examples of television exploring African Americans' deep emotional conflicts with regard to matters of love, marriage, ego, and assimilation.

Florida, steady and pragmatic, collided with Henry's fiercely proud but insecure firefighter (who moonlighted as a cabdriver) over the direction of their marriage and her insistence on being a housekeeper.

Maude offered a ready ear and constant moral support in an attempt to settle Florida's nerves. Florida, never much of a believer in this feminist mishegoss, was, however, swayed by Maude's strong pro-woman stances. This happened much to the consternation of her husband, Henry.

"We argued so bad this morning, Mrs. Findlay, there was even the threat of violence," laments Florida.

"Oh no, Florida!" retorts Maude.

"That's right and I ain't never hit him before."

It's easy to see the dynamic between Maude and Florida as a more thorough examination of Edith and Weezy, however, with their roles in society reversed. (Maude was also a more fully drawn version of Bunker's progressive feminist daughter, Gloria.)

In a dramatic living room showdown over Florida's job, a passionate and defiant Henry lays it out for all to see. Everything he's stood for as a man and a provider has led up to this moment.

"Let me tell you, baby, I'm ebony!" he begins. "In the world I grew up in a Black man couldn't even get a job, so the women had to go out and support the family. And quiet as kept, some of us never even wanted it that way. And some of us don't have to have it that way. Like me! Now, I got a J-O-B. And a good one. Now if I have to work two jobs then I will. Because I am no longer gonna be the husband of a Black maid!"

It's dramatic and raw and groundbreaking. That it takes place in Maude's upper-class living room is all the more disorienting. The audience does not know whether to clap or gasp and a smattering of applause is quickly drowned out by Florida's quip:

"You ain't gonna be sucked in by that jive, are you?"

Those who nervously clapped only made it more uncomfortable for those who hadn't. They are unsure where this is going. It's as if they are watching a private argument between a Black husband and wife pushed to the limit concerning topics those outside the community know little about.

It's her turn as she steps in front of Maude. Florida dives in:

> You're hurt because of your pride and I love you for that. But I also resent you for not being just as proud of me as I am of you. Your mother was a maid and that's how your brothers got through school and you got to be a fireman. There are a lot of women on both sides of my family who worked all their lives in white kitchens so their kids could get some of the things they should have. You want to be proud of something? You be proud of them because they was all Black women. And I tell you there ain't never been a better woman than that!

America loved what it saw and *Maude* quickly became a smash.

Thanks to the poignant, touching (and hilarious) relationship between Maude and Florida, the housekeeper's resiliency and sidesplitting comebacks, Esther Rolle quickly emerged as the show's most popular character.

As such, neither she nor Henry lasted long in the Findlay household. Lear quickly developed an idea for Florida and Henry to have their own show. He would hand the idea off to thirty-one-year-old African American writer Eric Monte and Michael Evans, who played George and Weezy's son, Lionel, on *All in the Family*. Monte and Evans would be the first African Americans credited with creating a sitcom.

The result in 1974, *Good Times*, wasn't a traditional spin-off so much as it was a showcase for Amos and Rolle. Florida and Henry were given entirely new backstories and the show was recentered on the South Side of Chicago—far from *Maude*'s upper-middle-class haven of Tuckahoe, New York. The couple raised a family of five in the Cabrini-Green housing project, where Eric Monte grew up.

(There was a time of pop cultural conversation of emptiness and intrigue—Did Florida and Maude miss each other? Did they wonder what had become of one another?)

Sanford & Son, starring comedian Redd Foxx as Fred Sanford, and *Julia*, starring Diahann Carroll, had preceded *Good Times* to air, but the Amos-Rolle sitcom was the first of its time to feature a two-parent, nuclear Black family. Notably, Lear had initially developed the show for Rolle alone, who would be a single mother to several children. But she refused to take the show unless the Evanses were a two-parent household. Rolle was the tenth of eighteen children in Pompano Beach, Florida, and her father had adamantly professed to her the need for America to see a portrayal of a complete Black family.

"I told Lear and the rest of the producers that I wouldn't compound the lie that Black fathers don't care about their children," Rolle said in *Ebony* magazine in 1978.

Still, Amos was riled up to no end about a show about

Black people in the projects that had no Black writers on staff except for Monte.

"I felt like I knew more about what a Black family should be and how a Black father would act than the writers, none of whom were Black," said Amos in a 2020 interview. "Their perception of what a Black family would be was different than mine. But mine was steeped in reality."

No problem was bigger than Amos and Rolle's beef with the character J.J., the Evanses' slack-jawed, layabout son. With his signature catchphrase "Dy-no-mite"—which young comedian Jimmie Walker initially ad-libbed—episodes began to revolve around his buffoonery.

"Let me say that I loved J.J. the character and Jimmie the actor," Lear wrote in his 2014 autobiography, *Even This I Get to Experience*. "In reality, they were not that far apart. The actor seemed to have shrugged off what was known as 'the black man's burden.' I believed that was the way he chose to deal with it. The man, the boy, was just plain funny. 'Dy-no-mite!' became a running joke, and the character of J.J., John and Esther began to believe, was running away with the show."

Lear's show devolved into constant disagreement between production and cast. Amos grew more distant. Rolle grew more and more vocal.

"[J.J. is] 18 and he doesn't work," said Rolle in a 1975 interview with *Ebony*. "He can't read or write, he doesn't think. The show didn't start out to be that."

Rolle considered the character a "jackass" and thought it made Black people look bad.

Still, the show was a hit.

But good times always end. And for everyone on the show, they ended badly.

Lear in *Even This I Get to Experience* on his battles with Rolle and Amos:

> I spoke of how much I'd learned in the process about the Black culture, for which I held such a deep affection and appreciation. I understood and respected why each of them felt entitled to their feelings about how their race should be represented on TV, reminded them of how many times even they disagreed, and then asked them to consider the problems these mind-sets were presenting to the creative staff, particularly me. Worst of all, I pointed out, this problem had started to affect our work, and we had to put an end to it.

In fits of anger over the direction of the show, Amos would challenge the writers to fisticuffs in the parking lot. They were sometimes afraid to be in the same room with him. On hiatus after the third season, Amos received a phone call from Lear.

"Hey, Big John, how ya doin'?" said Lear over the phone.

"I'm doing fine, what's up?" Amos replied.

"Well, I got good news and bad. The good news is we've been picked up for next season. The bad news is you won't be with us."

"How's that?" replied Amos.

"We had to let you go. We can't have you threatening the writers' lives."

Rolle would depart as well after the show's fourth season, resigning as she and Lear simply could not agree with what she felt was an increasingly inaccurate and destructive portrayal of urban Black life.

With its founding characters gone, the show's ratings sank, and it was quickly put on the cancellation block. One final attempt was made to save the program, with Rolle convinced to return in exchange for more control over how Black America was depicted in the program. She was also motivated by the opportunity to help save the jobs of the numerous Black actors it employed. But ultimately it wasn't enough, and its last episode aired in August 1979. It had been controversial, yes, but also a landmark for Black television. *Good Times* had run for six seasons in total, and its star Rolle earned three Emmy nominations for her work in the process. It remains one of the most critically important Black shows in television history.

But *Good Times*' denouement was far less celebratory. Co-creator Monte, who had stuck on staff as a writer through the third season before selling his screenplay for the 1974 film *Cooley High*, had been one of the loudest voices in the room as the Black cast members began to complain about its stereotypical content.

This had earned him a bad reputation with Lear and other producers, and the bad blood spilled into public over the years.

In 1977, Monte filed a $185 million lawsuit against CBS, ABC, Norman Lear, and Bud Yorkin. His claim was that he was denied credit and royalties for *Good Times*, *The Jeffersons*, and *What's Happening* (based on *Cooley High*). The suit was ultimately settled for $1 million in 1979 without any admission of wrongdoing by the companies, Lear, or Yorkin.

In the years after his departure from *Good Times*, Monte fell into a cycle of despair. He made a series of financial missteps and developed an addiction to crack cocaine. He found himself homeless, for a time taking up informal residence in Los Angeles's notorious MacArthur Park (the location detailed in the *Fresh Prince* episode "72 Hours" (Season One, Episode 23) before moving into a homeless shelter in Bell, California, in 2006.

Here is Monte in a 2006 interview at the Black Film and Media Conference, specifically talking about Lear: "Norman Lear is a racist and a hypocrite and a liar. I will state that emphatically. He's a thief and he's a liar."

The Huxtables Are Coming to Dinner

Brandon Tartikoff had convinced Bill Cosby to write a pilot. Despite Cosby's three failed attempts at a network sitcom, this one would result in the most successful Black show in network prime-time sitcom history and one of the most impactful television shows of all time.

(Given the accusations against and conviction of the

show's star Bill Cosby, and the exponential emotional fallout, for the sake of analysis this account will examine the show only as it was in the 1980s and its entertainment legacy. In no way is this meant to trivialize or minimize the suffering of those at the hands of its creator.)

Simply put, *The Cosby Show* changed television history.

NBC was last in the ratings before its arrival, and viewers were more focused on hour-long dramas like *Dynasty*, *Falcon Crest*, and *Dallas*. Even simpler fare like *The Incredible Hulk*, *Magnum P.I.*, and *The Dukes of Hazzard* proved more interesting to viewers and more profitable to networks.

Long before last-place NBC touted "Must See TV"—the most famous network tagline in history—it described its Thursday nights in press releases as "the best night in television." That night was anchored by the dramas *Fame* and *Hill Street Blues*.

For a November 1980 episode of *Dallas*—a CBS prime-time, Texas-based soap opera about greed and excess—titled "A House Divided," 76 percent of Americans tuned in—and 350 million around the world—to find out "who shot J.R." The cliffhanger episode from the previous season about the assassination attempt on the show's lead, a greedy, dashing, womanizing oil baron, captured the nation's attention like no program in history.

Networks tried in vain to duplicate that phenomenon with varying degrees of success but largely failed as American viewers' tastes shifted, unsurprisingly, yet again. The glut of melodramatic hour-long dramas had produced a need

for something new, much like the oversaturated age of the 1970s sitcom gave way to the tidal wave of early '80s prime-time dramas.

Brandon Tartikoff was thirty-four and had been NBC's president of entertainment for three years. He was obsessed with the television schedule and had committed to memory the lineup of every network. He was an obsessive who would even fiddle with his programming card at stoplights. Cars would often honk at his beat-up Volkswagen when he didn't see the light change.

At heart, the Yale grad was a comedy guy and would often look for talent in his own backyard. He watched *The Tonight Show* starring Johnny Carson nightly. He was tasked with finding a replacement for Carson and would take a keen interest in comics who would perform on the show. It was there that he first saw a young Jerry Seinfeld. He had taken a liking to Jay Leno, who often filled in as guest host.

One night Tartikoff was bushed and turned in early. But his screaming twelve-month-old, Calla, had other plans. To calm her down, Tartikoff sat her in front of the TV. And *The Tonight Show*. The guest was Bill Cosby, who charmingly went through a bit about the beautiful struggles of parenthood.

Within days Tartikoff was scrambling his ranks and firing off calls to set up a meeting and offered Cosby a pilot in the room. He credited Calla all the way.

"She usually goes to bed by eight," Tartikoff told the Associated Press a year later, "but on Thursday she wants to

watch 'Bill Cosberry.' Since she was part of the show's inspiration, we let her stay up the extra half hour."

It's hard to remember now, but *The Cosby Show* was a risk. America had never seen an ultrasuccessful, educated, grounded Black nuclear family like this. The Cosbys were in the economic one percent and dealing with real-world problems like suicide, unwanted pregnancy, and gun control with eloquence, aplomb, and other nouns not normally affixed to Black people.

America fell in love with Cosby's fractured but relatable take on fatherhood and family, with his unique brand of parenting doled out in equal parts wisdom and humor. Audiences rushed to find out the Huxtables' take on how to handle any given situation, and then went on to apply it to their own lives. What would Cliff tell his children? Would Claire approve?

Bill Cosby Became America's Dad

His sweaters became an iconic symbol of American fatherhood. His sometimes halting but matter-of-fact speech pattern meant you were hearing something important. No actor on an NBC show had ever scored higher with a test audience before a show aired than Bill Cosby. (Until Will Smith.)

His wife, Claire (Phylicia Rashad), was elegant and beautiful and regal. Strong and sure. Cherished by Cliff in a way a woman should be. He knew she was smarter. He knew when she was right. Women copied her hair, wanted to buy her

blouses, and started book clubs by the thousands because Claire had one. Oprah did, too.

His children were so different from one another—or any that American audiences were used to. They had the same problems as white kids in the burbs or flyover states or inner cities. They couldn't escape their problems on their own. They needed their parents' help.

There was the well-spoken, handsome Theo (Malcolm-Jamal Warner), who was obsessed with girls and sports cars while struggling with dyslexia.

The alluring, brooding, and artistic oldest daughter, Denise (Lisa Bonet), puzzled her parents with a revolving door of teenage drama and angst. Hearts melted when four-year-old Raven-Symoné was introduced as Olivia. She was equally capable of stealing a scene and hearts across the country.

The Cosby Show was a show about parenting. It was about teaching Black America. It was about showing white America what they didn't know about Black America. It was funny but people didn't tune in to laugh. They watched to feel connected. America saw themselves in a Black family without fully comprehending what a Black family could be.

It was a safe harbor. The Huxtables got through it. Which meant that maybe the viewer could, too. It was truly transcendent television.

It saved a network, a generation, a genre.

Tartikoff was willing to overlook nearly every obstacle that came with producing the show.

"It was an expensive show," he said. "It was in New York

and it had Bill's salary built into it. It was more expensive than we'd ever paid for any first-year, half-hour show."

In fact, Cosby and Tartikoff were so enamored of one another that the comedian once sent the network's president a telegram in which he explained that new ideas were percolating and jokingly asked for a seventh season.

"I'm sure that if Bill Cosby wants to come back," quipped Tartikoff, "it's not a problem for us."

(It was thought to be a joke, as *The Cosby Show* was No. 1 in the ratings at the time. It did, however, underscore Tartikoff's appreciation for talent and what it did for the network and his own legacy. Will Smith would soon be the beneficiary of that same affection.)

The success of the Cosby Experiment allowed Tartikoff to take risks on other experimental shows like *Seinfeld*, which would go on to surpass *Cosby* as NBC's biggest hit ever. And it was a big reason Tartikoff believed so much in Will. Especially after audience testing came in so high.

The Cosby Show revived the American sitcom, ran for eight seasons, and was nominated for fourteen Emmys, winning six, including Best Comedy Series in 1985. It solidified Tartikoff as a Hollywood titan.

By the time *Cosby* went off the air in 1992, in its wake *The Fresh Prince of Bel-Air* and ABC counterpart *Family Matters*, a wholesome show about an elevator operator and Chicago police officer's family, were in full stride. It marked the first time in television history that two highly rated Black family sitcoms ran simultaneously.

Other, less successful attempts did come—but none at the level of *Cosby*, *The Fresh Prince*, or the Urkel-fueled *Family Matters*. Fox's *227*, created by future *Fresh Prince* writer Bill Boulware, ran from 1985 to 1990 but largely focused on the comings and goings of residents of an apartment building and less so on a single family. *Roc*, starring the esteemed Charles S. Dutton, dealt with a Baltimore garbage collector and his extended family and ran from 1991 to 1994. The short-lived *Frank's Place*, starring Daphne Maxwell Reid, the second *Fresh Prince* Aunt Viv (Seasons Four–Six), combined drama and comedy with issues of class and race.

In the late 1990s and early 2000s, Black family sitcoms struggled to find footing but saw hits in *Parenthood*, *Everybody Hates Chris*, and *The Bernie Mac Show*. Almost all were anchored by comedians.

The closest spiritual successor to the writer-led sitcoms of the *Fresh Prince* era wouldn't arrive until 2014, in writer Kenya Barris's hit ABC sitcom *black-ish*. It is considered the standard-bearer of the portrayal of suburban Black life and has spawned spin-offs *grown-ish*, *mixed-ish, and old-ish*—making Barris the most prolific Black family sitcom creator since Norman Lear.

"On This Very Special Episode . . ."

Lompoc, a city along the rural central coast of California, is known by locals for two things: Federal Correctional Institution Lompoc and Vandenberg Air Force Base. The infamous prison led Vin Diesel's Dominic Toretto character in *The Fast and the Furious* to state, "I'll die before I go back." The latter is where the family of Winifred Celeste Hervey, army brat, causal jock, and soon-to-be prolific writer, were stationed thanks to her father Ramon's service.

Hervey was both bookish and athletic. Her father's military career during the time of the Cuban Missile Crisis and the Vietnam War sparked an interest in politics. Inspired by the children's novel *Harriet the Spy*, by Louise Fitzhugh, she began writing and keeping journals. At Cabrillo Senior High School she took creative writing, and she relished evenings around the family television set with her four siblings watching *The Jeffersons*, *All in the Family*, *I Spy*, and *Mission: Impossible*.

But she wasn't feeling *Good Times*.

"I used to hate that show," she said on the *Curry & Company* podcast in 2020. "Why did they have to be poor?"

But she loved Black representation on TV. Her grandmother would always announce to the family when there was a Black actor in a TV show. The entire brood would come running to the family room.

After a stint studying filmmaking at a junior college, she transferred to Loyola Marymount in Los Angeles to study television production and history. Through a program with the Academy of Television Arts & Sciences, she secured an internship on the television show *Rhoda*, starring Valerie Harper, then won a job as a staff writer on *Laverne & Shirley*, a spin-off of ABC's *Happy Days*.

However, her introduction to the television industry was more than rocky. Shortly after her arrival at Paramount, which produced *Laverne & Shirley*, her office was ransacked and many of her personal items were damaged. The word *nigger* was written on her scripts. She went to the executive producers to report the incident; they then raised the matter out in the open in front of the entire staff. Hervey was shocked at the insensitivity and left even more traumatized than she already had been.

She felt it impossible to trust her coworkers, thinking any one of them could be responsible.

A year later she joined *The Cosby Show* for the back nine

episodes of the first season. *Cosby* was the No. 1 show on television but not an environment that suited Hervey.

"It was a wonderful show to watch on TV," said Hervey, "but not a wonderful show to work on."

There were unwritten rules that weren't often clearly articulated. Once, when John Amos guest-starred he used the word *shit* between takes. The set fell silent. Phylicia Rashad quietly crept over to Amos.

"We don't use that kind of language around here," she whispered. Foul language had been expressly forbidden by Bill Cosby.

After the first season of *Cosby*, Hervey scored a meeting with Susan Harris, an ex-coworker at Robert Guillaume's *Benson*. Harris's new pilot, a quirky concept called *Golden Girls* and starring Bea Arthur and Betty White, had just been green-lit. Hervey jumped at an offer to hop over and worked there for three seasons, seventy-five episodes, and an Emmy Award for Outstanding Comedy Series. The show was a runaway hit—one of the happy experiences of Hervey's professional life. It also got her the attention of the new NBC president of entertainment, Warren Littlefield, who was looking for a replacement at *The Fresh Prince of Bel-Air* for the recently departed Borowitzes.

After a series of meetings and strong conversations with Smith and Quincy Jones, she was immediately offered the job. Hervey quickly endeared herself to cast members with her ready smile, soft disposition, and strong ideas.

They called her Winnie.

Her impact was immediate. She made upgrades to the set, including a new kitchen, living room, and furniture. The stairs were moved from the front foyer to the left rear of the family room, where they would remain until the show's final episode. Behind the couch were new double doors through which the actors could enter and exit. (She would also revamp the furniture in Season Three, adding a foosball table, a fireplace, and new vases.)

Her clever script for "Did the Earth Move for You?" (Season Two, Episode 1), guest-starring Tisha Campbell of *Martin* fame, was peppered with snappy dialogue and witty comebacks, a winning first writing credit on *The Fresh Prince*.

Will and his new girlfriend (Campbell) get stuck in the basement after an earthquake and the tension rises as he slowly discovers she's not who he thinks she is.

"I'm stuck in the basement sitting on a tricycle, girlfriend getting on my nerves," sings Will to the cadence of Prince's "Darling Nikki." "Going outta my mind, I thought she was fine, don't know if her body is hers."

Hervey was one of two African American female showrunners at the time of her hire. She could hang with the boys but quickly reminded them with as little as a knowing glance when to keep their distance.

She could be fierce. But she was a caring producer and was quite nurturing to young writers in whom she saw potential. She would also work aggressively, without emotion, to remove writers from her staff if she thought they didn't meet her standards. She worked in a world of men. This always presented certain complications. They thought she could be easily shouted down and overpowered, but this would prove to be false for the majority of her career.

Like most, she was taken with Will upon first meeting him.

"When he walks in a room you know it," Hervey told the Archive of American Television in 2016. "He's super charming and funny. He has IT, which crosses all lines. Everybody likes Will."

But their creative differences became apparent almost immediately. This was new territory for the twenty-one-year-old wunderkind Smith, whose power seemed to grow exponentially by the day. She would provide pushback to Will in a way the Borowitzes rarely did. The first disagreement came before they even started shooting the second season.

As Hervey recounted it, Smith inexplicably got the idea that he wanted to change the universally beloved opening credits and theme song. After a weeklong back and forth it was decided that the opening credit sequence would stay and would remain throughout the show's run.

A few episodes into the second season, Hervey and Smith were having a discussion off set before a taping when the audience caught a glimpse of Will and nearly in unison began rapping the opening theme song. Will smiled and perhaps for the first time realized the ubiquity of the song.

"Remember when I wanted to change that?" he said.

But Hervey loved Smith's creative instincts and how easily he could react on the fly and adjust to new ideas. He was fun to work with. But *The Fresh Prince* was Will's show and he had the most input.

Hervey: "He had say over everything."

Smith began to increasingly use the phrase "my show," which did not go unnoticed.

"That was sometimes problematic because he was the least experienced," said Hervey. "He was surrounded by a lot of experienced actors who had background in the theater so there was a certain kind of etiquette and that wasn't really his process."

"Striptease for Two" was one of Hervey's funniest shows as a writer. The elaborate, comical striptease performed by Alfonso Ribeiro in the episode was originally written for Will, but he didn't want to do it. When he wasn't feeling something, the conversation usually ended there.

Through determination and study, Smith's acting skills were rapidly improving. Will would constantly pick the brains of actors who worked on other shows. Once he got a hold of Denzel Washington's phone number and called the actor cold.

"Hi, this is Will Smith," he said. "I want to know everything you do."

The Oscar-winning actor obliged, imploring him to treat his work as a craft and take dramatic acting seriously for the first time.

His efforts were paying off and his confidence soared. He wanted to test his new skills with drama and heavier themes.

But Winnie didn't do issue shows. She didn't care about

"very special episodes." These were episodes that had become commonplace on network TV, in which a show would dramatically tackle a sensitive subject while doling out the appropriate amount of comedy.

"He always wanted me to do more serious shows," Hervey recalled. "That was a little bit of a philosophical difference that we had."

Hervey preferred shows like "The Alma Matter" (Season Three, Episode 18), where crooner Tom Jones visits Carlton in a dream as his guardian angel, with smoke billowing into the family room before he launches into a medley of his famous hits and, of course, breaks out the Carlton Dance.

"Oh my god, it's Tom Jones! What are you doing here?" asks Carlton.

"Well, I'm your guardian angel," replies Jones.

"No offense, Tom, but I always thought my guardian angel would be Black."

"Well, I knew Otis Redding," offers Jones.

It was funny but Will was getting antsy. Winnie was not interested. And wouldn't budge. That would be a problem. Not for Will. But for her.

Without question, Will's power had increased tenfold. The show was a hit. Movie directors regularly came calling. Smith was constantly in meetings on his lunch hour. Both he and his manager, James Lassiter, had designs on him becoming a huge movie star.

This was Will's show now.

"You Can't Tell Me No on My Own Show."

For anyone who joined the show midstride it was quickly made apparent, either through observation or being explicitly told, that *The Fresh Prince of Bel-Air* was Will's world and you were just visiting.

The job of fielding complaints or reining in Will often fell on Hervey. She had to put out constant fires, many of which she became engulfed in herself.

"I came in and all of a sudden I was working with a rapper," said Hervey. "A rapper with a posse. There were always so many people around. Some were in the writers' room, some were dancers, some were friends, and others I had no idea who they were.

"It was very political. You had to handle each situation delicately. Everyone wanted their voice heard. There were so many different factions wanting power."

Hervey came to be seen by many in Will's crew as someone who presented obstacles, someone who needed to be avoided at all costs. The clearest path to power was going behind her back.

He doesn't like some lady telling him what to do, Hervey thought. "There was a lot of arguing about how things should have been done."

Much in the way the show was molded around Will's talents, he had increasing say in everything from story lines to wardrobe, right down to the way the actors delivered their lines.

"Will wanted to have a say in everything," said Hervey. "He was allowed to give notes in a way other actors weren't."

The freedom afforded a newcomer particularly riled experienced members of the cast. James Avery was an experienced stage actor who had been working for twenty years. Janet Hubert was a classically trained dancer and singer with Broadway experience. Both constantly sought out Hervey to tweak the power dynamic on the set without upsetting Smith.

"They had to understand it's not *The Fresh Parents of Bel-Air*," said Hervey.

Smith and Hervey spent the better part of Season Two feeling each other out, like boxers in the opening round, before a flurry of jabs and uppercuts.

Will's slang was usually so specific to individual neighborhoods in Philly, Hervey often reasoned that audiences wouldn't get it. She felt *slimmies*, a term for young women Will pined for, and *mackin'*, the pursuit of said slimmies, would fall on deaf ears.

Smith was undeterred and rarely overruled. There were always bigger fish to fry, too, so producers didn't put excessive effort fighting the little battles.

One of Will's biggest contributions to *The Fresh Prince* was the emphasis on social issues, which would ultimately play a large part in defining the legacy of the show. Will railed against the idea of being just a comic cutout who spouts zingers and chases after women.

This was a huge point of conflict between Smith and

Hervey. "Will wanted to do issue shows," remembered Hervey. "I don't do issue shows."

Hervey continued to push back, trying to maintain some semblance of order on set, as Will continued to push to shape the show into a feature-film-ready showcase of his actorly talents and seriousness. The match came to a standstill, until the world tipped things irreversibly in Will's favor.

In early March 1991, a motorist named Rodney King was stopped for speeding in the San Fernando Valley and beaten viciously by four members of the Los Angeles Police Department. The attack was caught on camera in grainy footage by a bystander from his balcony.

It shocked the country, sparked international outrage, and fourteen months later saw the four officers put on trial for the beating in a Simi Valley, California, courtroom. After seven days of deliberation the jury returned a not-guilty verdict.

The Los Angeles Riots ensued.

The city was locked down.

Sixty-three people were killed. Nine of them were shot by police officers.

More than twelve thousand people were arrested in six days. Nearly all of them were Black or Latino, despite the fact that African Americans made up just 6 percent of California's population, according to the 1990 census.

The Fresh Prince had just broken for summer hiatus, wrapping the final episode of Season Two on May 4—the episode in which Will refused to perform the striptease—marking the end of Winnie's first season as showrunner.

As the city exploded in a maelstrom of anger, frustration, and violence, Smith watched from his home in Philly. He was deeply affected by television images of his adopted city burning to the ground.

Upon the show's return in September 1992, Smith immediately suggested an episode to reflect the riots.

"Will Gets Committed" (Season Three, Episode 2) centers on the Banks family returning to their roots in the South Central section of Los Angeles to help clean up the block they once called home before moving on up to Bel-Air.

The episode contains a black-and-white flashback that shows the Banks family about ten years younger, living in a cramped apartment with few amenities and no butler. Glimpses of their future personalities are on display for comedic effect.

It's the first time *Fresh* mentions the Bankses' coming from relative poverty, a history that seems oddly incongruent with the career path of a successful Princeton-educated lawyer. What's more, we see Hilary as a spoiled ten-year-old with a Valley Girl cadence, odd behavior coming from someone who we now find was born in Compton. Carlton asks Uncle Phil to read him the *Wall Street Journal* as a bedtime story. Will pops in at nine years old, which is counter to the idea of his first trip to Los Angeles being when his mother sent him to live with his auntie and uncle in Bel-Air.

Will, correctly, thought the scene didn't work. It was too camp and the timelines didn't match at all. He immediately voiced his disapproval to Hervey.

"I'm not feeling it," said Will. "Let's get rid of it. Just delete that scene."

"I think the scene works fine," countered Hervey.

Will curled his lip and let out a slow breath.

"You can't tell me no on my own show," he said.

"I think I just did."

"Good, you can call me when you change your mind."

Word quickly spread that Will had walked off the set, despite the fact it was his day off. Hervey, sensing a fast-building storm, called the network. She explained that Will was unhappy with the scene and wanted it removed.

"I know," the network exec responded. "Will already called."

The decision was made to show the scene to a group of executives who would then vote on whether or not to delete it. The execs loved it and decided it would remain. After the episode aired, UCLA's film department requested it for their archives.

The decision was a rare defeat for Smith, and a satisfying victory for Hervey. But it did not come without a price. Hervey had to now exercise great caution in picking her battles. Will's crew would certainly be circling the wagons.

Hervey knew she should tread lightly but it simply wasn't in her nature. A producer had to be authoritative. Further conflict with Will would surely be met with staunch resistance and she would run the risk of exhausting her precious political capital.

And this was only Episode 2.

At the end of the season Hervey met with her agent and set up a meeting with the network to discuss her contract for the next season. The network was pleased with her work, as she had written some of the season's best episodes. They wanted her back. With a raise. But there was a catch.

"The network wanted me to produce the show from my office," said Hervey. "There was just no way I was doing that."

That would be like asking a coach to coach the team from the locker room. It would effectively strip her of essential duties and make interacting with the cast a chore. Out of sight, out of mind. It was a demotion in disguise.

Simply put . . . Hervey was outnumbered. No matter how clever her dialogue was.

She was told Will didn't want her there. So Winifred Hervey left the show.

● ● ●

Shortly thereafter, award-winning director Stan Lathan asked Hervey to help develop a series for comedian Steve Harvey. The resulting *The Steve Harvey Show*, in which Hervey was credited as creator and executive producer, ran for six seasons and 122 episodes. She became the second African American woman to develop her own prime-time series, behind Yvette Lee Bowser (*Living Single*), who like Hervey was an alum of *The Cosby Show* and was coincidentally a teenage friend of future *Fresh Prince* cast member Karyn Parsons.

Hervey speaks with reverence about Smith today and

remembers her time on *The Fresh Prince* fondly. But Hervey was not the only woman who would seem to have a high-profile, harrowing exit at the end of Season Three.

Gary H. Miller would become the show's third showrunner in four seasons, beginning with the 1993–94 season. And with that came a whole new set of problems.

A storm was brewing.

The Pregnant Aunt of Bel-Air

The show was a runaway ratings smash. In 1992, *The Cosby Show* had concluded its run and *Seinfeld* was still struggling to find its footing. The quality of *The Fresh Prince* episodes had risen steadily and the show was the hit NBC could ride to syndication.

While the cast got along famously on-screen, their television chemistry masked the storm that was brewing beneath the surface.

Hubert had a laundry list of complaints about Will that seemed to grow exponentially and more caustic with each passing episode. There was nothing that Will could do that didn't irk Hubert.

The complaints started first thing in the morning. When Will would arrive for work you could hear him a block away blasting his music. When he pulled into the parking lot, Hubert fumed that the bass was so thunderous it would rattle her dressing room window.

Hubert claims Will had it in his contract that no other actors from *The Fresh Prince* were allowed to appear on *The Tonight Show* during the first season other than Will. It's a dubious claim given the haphazard fashion in which Will's contract was drawn up in Quincy's driveway for a show that did not yet exist. But Hubert would make this claim for years.

Herself an accomplished dancer and thespian who wore a willful pride, Hubert maintains that Will's ego was inflated by the fact that he was the star of the show and rarely responded to notes, those bits of suggestion or direction that can sometimes agitate an actor.

"Janet is a woman of very strong emotions," said Susan Borowitz. "So if she loves you she's hugging the life out of you. But she couldn't understand her role. When a star like Will is born, no matter how good the show is around them they are the center of the universe. That's what riled Janet."

She felt she wasn't getting the love, adulation, and respect from the production she felt she deserved. Not even award season helped.

Hubert became the first actor from *The Fresh Prince* to be nominated for her work on the show when she got the nod for Outstanding Supporting Actress in a Comedy Series at the NAACP Image Awards in 1991. (Smith received two Golden Globe nominations for Best Performance by an Actor in a TV Series–Comedy/Musical but lost to John Goodman [*Roseanne*] in 1993 and Jerry Seinfeld [*Seinfeld*] in 1994.)

Nothing seemed to agitate Hubert more than what she perceived as Will's constant need to live up to his reputation as the life of the party. She was particularly vexed when she felt Smith's humor would cross from playful digs to mean-spirited and downright disrespectful.

Often before the show Will would come out before taping and warm up the audience. He would ping-pong back and forth with lighthearted roasting of audience members and "Yo mama" jokes, punctuated by exaggerated facial expressions.

One afternoon, Hubert recalled, Will reeled off a half dozen or so "Yo mama" jokes:

Yo mama's so black, she can leave fingerprints on charcoal.

Yo mama's so black, she went to night school and got marked absent.

Yo mama's so black that lightning bugs follow her in the daytime.

Yo mama's so black, I shot her and the bullets came back with flashlights saying, "I can't find the bitch."

The audience howled. Janet's blood boiled. As a darker-skinned African American woman, who was strong-willed both on-and off-screen, she felt attacked and disrespected. At forty-one, she still carried the scars from name calling and the humiliation of losing out on jobs based on her skin color.

Hubert felt Will held a bias against dark-skinned women

and that his girlfriends on the show "could never be darker than the bottom of Smith's foot."

Rumors persisted that Smith was annoyed that Hubert didn't laugh at his jokes when the cast sat around riffing and busting on one another. Or worse, during read-throughs.

Making matters worse was the fact that Hubert was pregnant and her changing body zapped her confidence and bravado. She had put on thirty-five pounds and could no longer wear her own shoes. She claims her access to the set was limited and that she was told to confine herself to her dressing room when not filming, where she would often break down and cry. She was constantly on the brink of tears and would burst into them a dozen times a day.

Her agent told her that Smith had gone to the network telling them that Hubert's silence made him uncomfortable and she was to keep her distance. Whether it was true or not hardly mattered. It mattered because she thought Will said it. And one did not simply win these kinds of battles against Will Smith.

Hubert felt Smith did not respect her delicate condition and had become generally an inconsiderate person. The actress accused Will and Alfonso of making fun of her weight gain without so much as trying to hide it.

What's more, while she loved the work that makeup artist Joann Kozloff did, Hubert was miffed that there were no Black makeup artists on staff. During her pregnancy she got into a shouting match with Kozloff for doing a poor job on her makeup and making what she felt were insensitive comments.

"Your job is to know when I look like shit on camera!" she shouted.

She thought Will was threatened by strong women and had very little respect for women in general. Hubert, who came from Broadway, would repeatedly say Will didn't understand camaraderie among actors because he was a rapper.

Then story lines became a problem for Hubert. She resented the lack of progression in her character, thinking she had gone from a professor to just a well-dressed housewife. Even though she was at odds with Ribeiro, she thought his character had become a "village idiot." In "A Funny Thing Happened on the Way Home from the Forum" (Season Three, Episode 11), which starred Vanessa Williams as Will's favorite sportswriter who attends a Lamaze class with Vivian and develops a crush on her, Hubert couldn't understand why Philip, with whom she already shared three children, didn't attend the class. She also found it in poor taste that Will would flirt with a married woman who was eight months pregnant.

"How dare I argue with the writers who seemed neither to understand the culture of Black womanhood," Hubert wrote in her 2008 self-published book, *Perfection Is Not a Sitcom Mom*. "Who the hell did I think I was? I was committing professional suicide. I wasn't just shooting myself in the foot. I was slitting my own throat. Just give me the knife. Allow me!"

(In "Home from the Forum" [Season Three, Episode 11], there appears to be a palpable tension, little chemistry, and a sense that Hubert is trying to hide, which has a noticeable effect on her performance. She seems distant, absent, and distracted.)

During the show's third season, Hubert's relationship with Smith had become too icy to bear or hide. They didn't speak when they passed each other in the hallway and never ate lunch together anymore. She fretted over what she thought was Will's network of "spies."

"If there is one thing Will can't stand, one thing that is his weakness," said Hubert, it is that "he needs to be liked or believe he is the nicest human being on the planet. His ego demands it."

She began to withdraw and the number of story lines revolving around Aunt Viv began to decline as she got deeper into her pregnancy. She countered that Will and Alfonso were spreading false rumors about her private life and ordering the crew not to speak to her. Going to showrunner Winifred Hervey wouldn't do much good, as she was locked in her own political struggles and siding with Hubert would surely seal her own fate.

On February 22, 1993, Hubert appeared in "The Baby Comes Out" (Season Three, Episode 20), then she missed the next two episodes recovering from her pregnancy and nursing her infant son, Elijah. She returned for the second-to-last show of the season, "The Way We Were" (Season Three, Episode 23), a clip show reliving the family's adventures with a deli-sliced-thin story about Philip and Vivian renewing their vows despite the fact Uncle Phil has lost his wedding ring.

The cast drags itself through the lifeless scenes absent

the energy and comedic oomph the show had come to be known for, looking like they wished they were as far from Sunset Gower Studios as possible. On IMDb, the episode holds the lowest audience score of any of the seventy-three *Fresh Prince* episodes to that point. Hubert appears in just the last ninety seconds, in a backyard ceremony revealing she's had possession of the ring. She has just one line in the show.

"I took it to get it inscribed," says Vivian, "for a hundred years more."

Her voice is weak and wavers on the last few words. It would be Janet Hubert's final line on *The Fresh Prince of Bel-Air*. She was not written into the final episode of Season Three.

Down Goes OG Aunt Viv

Shortly after Hubert gave birth, she went to NBC in Burbank with her agent to meet with network executives to discuss her future. She was excited about the arrival of her new baby, and even though her home life had been rife with what she alleged was emotional and physical abuse, she was ready for a fresh start. Season Four would be different. She just knew it.

But the meeting at NBC was tense from the start. She felt the executives were dismissive and deceptive. She had zero trust in the suits and it showed.

From her book *Sitcom Mom:*

"Look, we know he can be a pain in the ass some-times," the network suits said. "But he is the star of the show."

"That's cool," I said. "The name is his, but my life isn't." A little bird should have grabbed my tongue and snatched it out of my throat. But no; I went on. "So being on time is what I know and as long as he does that I don't give a damn."

"Then we are in agreement," said the suits. "Let's have a good season. And by the way you look great."

They were plotting my death at that very moment while smiling their overpaid network smiles.

In late May the network returned to Hubert with an offer. She would appear in just ten of the twenty-four episodes and take a pay cut of over $100,000. She was also barred from guest-starring on other shows—a vital source of income for working actors. The offer felt to Hubert like an insult. Moreover, it wouldn't be enough to cover her living expenses. Hubert had accrued massive debt. She had gotten a new house and taken out a multiyear lease on a new exercise studio. Not to mention the expenses of a newborn baby.

Her husband was out of work—she was also support-ing his daughter from a previous marriage—and Hubert felt alone and trapped and on the verge of a nervous breakdown.

She felt that Smith, NBC, and other unseen forces were destroying her career in front of her eyes.

"Do You Think She Should Go?"

After Season Three ended Joseph Marcell returned to London and was preparing to resume his work with the Royal Shakespeare Company when he got a call from Will Smith, he explained to Viral Hip-Hop News. After exchanging a few pleasantries Will got to the point.

"What do you think about Janet?" Smith asked. "Do you think she should go?"

"You have to do what you have to do," replied Marcell. "Sit down and iron out your differences."

Next James Avery called, asking what he thought.

"I cannot think, I don't have an opinion," Marcell informed him. "I will not put the knife in her but I will tell the truth."

Then Janet finally called. She was close with Marcell but explained her true frustration for the first time. She was confused, hurt, and angry. Marcell was direct.

"You have to look at it the way it's set up," Marcell recalled telling her. "It's Will's show. Don't create a political impasse because in the end you are the one who's going to suffer.

"Success corrupts. It eats at you. It does not bring contentment and satisfaction. It asks how much is enough. And so you are never satisfied."

After much discussion, the network made the ten-episode offer. Hubert had just two weeks to accept. Hubert thought about the arrangement for a few days and declined the offer. Several days later she changed her mind and told the producers that she wished to continue, but she was rebuffed. The offer was no longer on the table.

Hubert desperately needed this job. She called Will repeatedly. He never picked up. Janet begged Karyn Parsons to talk to Will, knowing the two had a strong relationship.

Will was incensed that Janet insisted that he orchestrated her ouster. Three months after *The Fresh Prince*'s series finale he tried to clear the air in an August 1996 issue of *Ebony* magazine in which Smith appeared on the cover:

> Janet Hubert-Whitten was an incredible actress. She brought so much spirit and warmth and fun to *The Fresh Prince of Bel-Air*. She made that set a home. Of course there was pain in her not returning to the show and all that, but there was the thing that she thought it was me. That kind of irritated me but people will make their own beds and they are going to have to sleep in them. I didn't have anything to do with it. She just never believed that. I think the show suffered with the loss of Janet Hubert.

Hubert was irate: "What was this? It was a little too late. Besides, what Hollywood executive reads *Ebony*? He didn't put it across the wire service like all of the other crap he did. He turned into a pit bull at the time and tore my ass to shreds."

She suspected Ribeiro was instrumental in planting a

damaging story in the *Globe* about her stalking Smith, although there was no proof this was true.

After Hubert left the show, Smith went on a publicity tour designed to kill her career, according to the actress. She says Winifred Hervey told her the network even asked Will to stop.

"You were a dead body," Hubert says Hervey told her. "You were expendable."

Hubert spent forty thousand dollars that she didn't have on a single lawyer after filing a wrongful termination suit against NBC and Smith, saying she was forced off the show due to her pregnancy.

Smith came equipped with nine network lawyers, who peppered Hubert in a nine-hour deposition about her finances, marriage, mental state, family, children, "Yo mama" jokes, and even her pets.

Smith's attorneys asked her about the term *high yellow*.

Hubert lost nearly all her friends from the show and as much weight to match. Arbitration ruled against her. She was nearly $100,000 in debt and defaulted on her exercise studio lease. Her marriage had reached a breaking point and after her divorce she was forced to sell her house and move into a small apartment. Her friend from the Broadway days Angela Bassett came over, Scotch tape gun in hand, to help her pack her things and loaned her money to get set up in a studio apartment.

What followed would be a twenty-seven-year public feud between Hubert and Smith.

"You're Still My Aunt Viv"

Smith, in the 2021 telling of his complex and extraordinary life, in his 423-page autobiography *Will*, mentions Hubert by name only once and doesn't allude to the decades-long standoff. But Smith had begun to publicly soften around 2017 as Hubert continued to lob emotional mortars at the star by way of morning show appearances and Facebook posts. Cracks began to show in the seemingly unending impasse, which completely collapsed in November 2020 when Hubert agreed to appear on HBO Max's *The Fresh Prince of Bel-Air Reunion* for a tearful face-to-face in an attempt to soothe wounded egos and bury the painful past for good. But most importantly, to apologize.

"You hurt me," said Hubert.

"When I left the show, I had this new baby and no one," said Hubert. "Family disowned me. Hollywood disowned me. My family said, 'You've ruined our name.'

"You took all that away from me with your words," she told Smith. "Words can kill. I lost everything. Reputation. Everything, everything. I understand you were able to move forward.

"I wasn't unprofessional on the set; I just stopped talking to everybody, because I didn't know who to trust, because I had been banished. But you know those words, calling a Black woman 'difficult' in Hollywood is the kiss of death. It's the kiss of death, and it's hard enough being a dark-skinned Black woman in this business, but I felt it was necessary for us to finally move forward."

"The person I want to be is someone who protects you," Smith said, dabbing the tears in his eyes, "not someone that unleashes dogs on you."

On January 13, 2022, Janet Hubert's sixty-sixth birthday, Will posted a two-picture tribute to Hubert—one regal and reflective, the other a nostalgia-inducing publicity shot of the two before *The Fresh Prince* even aired—to his Instagram, which boasts 57.7 million followers.

He wrote: "Happy BDay Janet! Blessings on another trip around the sun :-)"

It has been liked more than 700,000 times.

At the end of their emotional reunion, Hubert reached out and gently touched his chin with the softest touch and an exquisite amount of love.

Just as she had done on the day they met.

A tear fell.

"You're still my aunt Viv."

"They Ain't Never Met
a Nigga Like Me"

It wasn't that hard for Devon Shepard not to fit in. Rarely does someone from South Central find himself on a writing staff of a network show. NBC's Burbank offices were twenty-six miles and seventeen exits away from the battle-scarred streets of Compton. He knew those streets well—lined with liquor stores and burned-out buildings.

For some reason there were no banks or flower shops or yoga studios there. If you didn't have a car you didn't get to a grocery store, unless you braved that crowded-ass bus. Maybe the nearest was in Koreatown or on Alvarado or a block that hadn't been taken over by the Rollin' 40s Crips, or worse, the notoriously brutal cops from Rampart.

Children bought juice and candy with change when they were sent to the store for cigarettes and beer.

The sidewalks were without tree cover and shade. City planning had not yet come to one of Los Angeles's oldest neighborhoods, is the guess. Sun-blasted, working-class Black people waited at bus stops. The city doesn't plant trees in the hood.

They don't repair the uneven sidewalks from root systems of trees they cut down twenty years ago, either. Grandmothers walked home on those jagged sidewalks, from storefront to storefront, bus shelter to church service, careful to navigate.

Perpetually bathed in blue and red lights. "POP, POP, POP" at 3 a.m. its reliable soundtrack.

It shaped Shepard's DNA. His every outlook on life.

Without any idea of how to make it in show business, he used a fortuitous connection and genuine street hustle to change his life. He was crazy about TV and movies and wanted to tell stories of his own. One day he crossed paths in a barbershop with a thirty-two-year old *Fresh Prince* writer, Rob Edwards.

They shot the shit, and Edwards saw something in the kid with the big dreams and ever-bigger ideas. He told him he'd talk to his partners, none other than Andy and Susan Borowitz. They were two years removed from *The Fresh Prince* and the trio had teamed up to recently sell a sitcom pilot called *Out All Night,* starring Patti LaBelle and Vivica A. Fox, still to star alongside Smith in *Independence Day.*

"They're going to need to see a sample," said Edwards. "They want you to write a script."

"What's a script?" replied Shepard.

Oh boy. Edwards explained the basics—beginning, middle, end—and Shepard knocked something together. The format was jacked up and it was all over the place. But there was something there. Through the errors and his inexperience and roughness they could see a diamond.

He was brought on as a writer's trainee for *Out All Night*. It was a glorified internship but he was in the door. He quickly got the hang of the day-to-day of the show, the nuts and bolts of scriptwriting, and stayed late often.

Right away producers liked his gritty, unfiltered take and the energy he brought to the writers' room. He didn't know a key grip from a keyhole but was hungry to learn. He was quickly bumped up to staff writer and wrote three episodes during the show's first season, earning a rep for balancing laughs with gravitas. But on July 9, 1993, the show was canceled after just twenty episodes.

Since the show was produced by NBC (and Quincy Jones), he was already on their radar and scored a meeting with the network the following week, and with Edwards's help he landed a spot on the writing staff of *The Fresh Prince* for Season Four.

After Winifred Hervey's tumultuous exit several weeks earlier, the network made the decision to hire writers before installing a new showrunner. The inherent danger was that the eventual boss on set wouldn't embrace the staff because they hadn't been handpicked. Sort of like a newly hired head coach who didn't get to select his assistant coaches. But NBC eventually settled on Gary H. Miller, a veteran sitcom producer whom Shepard, obviously, had never heard of.

The experience at *The Fresh Prince* was a culture shock for Shepard. He was young, Black, and brash, and carried around a rather large chip on his shoulder. As just one of four Black writers on a staff that numbered eighteen, he quickly found his cultural and political views and attitudes toward race did not mesh with anyone in the room.

He likened the experience to high school. There were the cool kids, nerds, jocks, and class clowns, he thought. And of course the smart-asses. But Shepard was the most politically aggressive.

"It was just like being at the lunch table," Shepard told me. "It could be petty but you just had to find someone you got along with. Back then there was no HR to run to and a lot of times you just got shit off your chest if there was an argument."

With Shepard in the room there could be heated clashes. He was twenty-two and still living at home with his mother in South Central on Ninety-First Avenue. His dark skin made people feel uneasy and his sharp tongue often served as a bullwhip. His hair was braided and despite a quick, dry wit he rarely smiled. He wore excessively baggy clothes and sported a pager on his hip.

He even occasionally sold dope on the side despite earning eight thousand dollars a week from writing on the show.

But what irked his colleagues most was that he listened to Louis Farrakhan and became increasingly vocal about his views on race relations.

When a group of Jewish *Fresh Prince* writers found out that Shepard had gone to see Farrakhan speak in person, their reactions ranged from alarmed to furious. The following Monday he was cornered by the group, who demanded an explanation. They led him to a conference room and surrounded him on all sides, Shepard explained.

"I was sitting down in a chair and eight guys completely surrounded me," he said. "I wasn't scared. I held my ground. I handled my business and let them know how I felt."

Over the course of an hour voices were raised, exceptions taken.

No quarter was asked. None given. But there was anger and mistrust on both sides.

Shepard felt the writers were entitled, elitist, out of touch. The writers thought Shepard was bullheaded and ignorant. Many had Ivy League pedigrees, wrote at the *Harvard Lampoon* or a humor paper of some record. On this day they could not come to an agreement. But a truce was reached. When they emerged from the room, tempers cooled and at the very least they weren't at each other's throats.

For now. Mostly, Shepard felt he had earned respect for articulating his point.

"I held my ground," said Shepard. "They ain't never met a nigga like me."

This caught the attention of staffer Bill Boulware, a forty-two-year-old African American writer from Harlem who was a lifelong scribe. In the 1980s he had created the hit show *227* but was subsequently blacklisted for aggressively espousing Black Power views. By 1993, the year Shepard joined *The Fresh Prince*, he had worked his way back to a writers' room.

One afternoon Boulware witnessed an argument where Shepard had threatened to take another writer out to the parking lot and deliver the beatdown of his life. After the would-be combatants were separated, Boulware immediately told Shepard he was taking him to lunch. An hour later they arrived at Le Dome, a trendy West Hollywood spot once owned by Elton John. After ordering a couple of steaks, Boulware sipped his water and proceeded to rip into Shepard.

"I brought you here to tell you that you're fucking up," said Boulware firmly. "You're blowing your potential."

The dressing-down had a huge impact on Shepard. The older man was forceful yet restrained. He believed in the upstart. Boulware gave his respect unequivocally. Shepard had never had someone care about him so angrily, yet so paternally. The moment would mark the beginning of a lifelong mentorship.

"He checked me like I never been checked before," remembered Shepard. "He told me to knock it off, which saved my career."

Shepard got the message. He adjusted his attitude. He cut his hair. Shaved it off at his mom's house that night. He left the chip on his shoulder on the side of the road. He wanted this thing to work. Writers would continue to knock heads but the disagreements were usually related to creative ideas and would be peacefully resolved with enough diplomacy. That was the nature of having so many talented and opinionated writers working in a pressure cooker while trying to keep their heads above water.

Despite the flare-ups and renewed perspectives, there was work to be done. The work never stopped.

But something happened. Something that they could not intend.

Devon Shepard and Bill Boulware would each write the two most important episodes in *Fresh Prince* history.

"I Thought He Was Corny"

On Mondays writers would crowd into the large conference room on the second floor and begin tossing out ideas. When one caught steam and got laughs and support it would begin to be shaped into a full-fledged story. The writer who originally pitched the idea to the group would then turn it into a written pitch and send it off to the showrunner.

If there was interest he'd be asked to write a thorough outline. He would break the story: come up with and arrange each individual scene for that story.

Upon approval from showrunner Miller, and some notes from the network, the writer had the green light to begin writing the episode.

Given his background, Shepard wanted to write about

themes that related to Black culture. These ideas were often rebutted by white writers who weren't interested or simply didn't understand.

The days of Andy and Susan Borowitz exploring Black culture, consulting Black writers, and demonstrating an openness to learn on *The Fresh Prince* were long past.

During a pitch meeting a couple of writers pitched an idea where Carlton joins a white fraternity. Will and Carlton would assume the fraternity was racist but that notion only ended up being their own misunderstanding.

Led by Shepard, the Black writers quickly pushed back, rankling a group of white writers.

"How come Black people have to be the ones that misunderstand racism?" demanded Shepard. "Why do we have to pretend racism doesn't exist?"

It boiled over into a huge argument.

"Fuck it," said Shepard. "Let's find some middle ground."

They agreed to have Will and Carlton join a Black fraternity. The only problem was that the frat didn't think Carlton was Black enough. The kicker: Carlton would finally have to stand up for himself.

"You're gonna have those disagreements but if you're in a creative space you can turn that into something really cool," said Shepard.

After using humor to mock Carlton's perceived level of acceptable Blackness for three seasons, almost exclusively at the hands of Will's character, this episode would hit the topic head-on.

Jokes would be replaced by serious social commentary and explore the reality of Black people judging one another by their own varied, often flawed definitions of Blackness. And there would be the fallout of the resulting pushback. Carlton would no longer be able to shrug it off in service of the next joke.

Many of the *Fresh Prince* ideas were plucked from the writers' real-life experiences, whether they were innocuous observations, awkward dates, professional disappointments, or broader themes from their childhoods. Shepard's life experience, his opinion of Ribeiro, and the angst in the writers' room would become "Blood Is Thicker than Mud" (Season Four, Episode 17), Shepard's first writing credit on *The Fresh Prince*.

Shepard had enough self-awareness to know that a lot of the tension in the office was a result of his misgivings and distrust of those he considered different. Just about everyone was soft to him.

In no case was that more true than with Alfonso Ribeiro.

"When I first met Alfonso I thought he was corny," said Shepard. "Because my Blackness was monolithic at the time. I'm thinking that he needs to be like me—same shared experience, same shared trauma. But he had such an eventful and interesting life."

A revelation: Shepard let his guard down.

"Then we just started hanging out and I realized he's a dope motherfucker. I mean he was special how he carried himself. How he treated others. I couldn't have been more wrong about somebody. He was probably even more secure in himself than I was."

When Shepard let his guard down the writer and the actor began to form a friendship. After work Shepard would jump in his 1993 Nissan 300ZX and race over to Denzel Washington's restaurant, Georgia's, on Melrose to nosh on chicken fingers or sushi. Afterward it was down the street to the hole-in-the-wall speakeasy, Creeque Alley, with its dim lighting and spicy Jamaican patties, to knock back a few drinks.

It would be packed with actors, rappers, and Lakers. People would dance on tables. It was five deep at the bar most nights. Dr. Dre would pull up and grab a booth in the back. Snoop Dogg was so young they didn't recognize him.

He watched as Ribeiro so easily moved in virtually any surrounding. He was kind to the valet. Cracked jokes with the bartender. Effortlessly chatted up the most beautiful girl in the room. He could be quizzical, pensive, or thoughtful. He could conjure up bravado or blend in without pretense or ego. He could talk a mean competitive game on the golf course. He was a team player but could steal the spotlight in an instant, then simply return it without a word, so you could shine, too.

He was also Black. He wasn't part of Shepard's monolith. He neither reinforced nor tarnished Shepard's identity or view of himself. At the same time he didn't need anyone to participate in his own self-perception.

"He just knew who he was," remembered Shepard. "I was impressed."

The Real Sellout

By Wednesday of that week's schedule, Shepard had knocked the script into shape so the actors could get it up on its feet in rehearsals.

As with most every adventure on *The Fresh Prince*, Will and Carlton are joined at the hip. After having settled reasonably well into college life, it is time to embark on a rite of passage together. They both decide to pledge Phi Beta Gamma, the most influential Black fraternity on the campus of the fictional University of Los Angeles.

Will and Carlton have been busting their butts through four long weeks of hazing to prove their worthiness and impress the frat's president, Top Dog, played by Glenn Plummer, fresh off his role in *Menace II Society* opposite Smith's future wife, Jada Pinkett.

At an on-campus party celebrating the completion of their running of a most humiliating gauntlet, they finally get the news they've been waiting for.

"You've got nothing to worry about," says Top Dog to Will. "You're in."

"Yo, word! Me and Carlton got in?" asks an excited Will.

"Well, not exactly," Top Dog informs him. "You're cool and all but Carlton is not exactly our type."

Across the room, Carlton is in the middle of the whitest dance possible as a gaggle of bemused coeds looks on.

"What do you mean not our type?" asks a dejected Will.

"Carlton doesn't exemplify what I think a Phi Beta

229

Gamma is. It's not Ralph Lauren shirts, wing-tipped shoes, and corporate America. We don't need a brother like him in this fraternity."

"Carlton is exactly what you need. He gives you one hundred and fifty percent every time!" exclaims Will before walking away angrily.

Will grabs Carlton and tells him they didn't get in. As they begin to leave the party, Carlton demands to know why Top Dog has rejected Will.

"We want Will," Top Dog says. "It's you we don't want."

Carlton is crushed.

"But I did everything," he says as his head hangs.

"Everything your butler does for you. I'm not accepting no Bel-Air-bred sellout into my fraternity."

Carlton has been wounded yet again by someone else's definition of Blackness being thrust on him while he is simultaneously dismissed.

Will steps in but Carlton insists on standing on his own two feet.

"Will, I got this."

It's the first time in the show where Carlton has directly hit this topic head-on. This is ultimately a battle that neither Will nor anyone else can fight for him. The studio is pin-drop quiet.

Carlton turns to Top Dog: "You think I'm a sellout. Why? Because I live in a big house and dress a certain way? Being Black isn't what I'm trying to be, it's what I am. I'm running the same race and jumping the same hurdles you are, so why are you tripping me up? You said we need to stick together but you don't even know what that means. If you ask me, you're the real sellout."

It is a profound moment. Carlton is no longer simply the butt of jokes. He is becoming a man. In a larger, at the time unknown conundrum, the show could no longer return to cheap, fast quips about race and Blackness.

It never would.

"Black Like Me"

During rewrites a producer suggested Carlton's speech be given to Will. Shepard was strongly opposed.

"I wanted Alfonso to have that moment based on my experience with him," said Shepard. "Me writing that for him was my way of righting the wrong. The way I treated him."

When the boys arrive home they inform Uncle Phil that they didn't make the cut.

"I have worked very hard to give my family a good life," says a nearly muted yet exasperated Uncle Phil. "When are we going to stop doing this to each other?"

The penultimate scene is Carlton's most riveting monologue on a subject that has plagued him in most of his adult experiences with Black people.

For the first time, Carlton owns his Blackness.

He defines it. No one else.

This episode was the most uphill battle since the Borowitzes left. Director Shelley Jensen, who directed the frat house episode, never wanted to stray too far away from the show's original laugh-out-loud ethos.

"The actors were always on board with the special shows but I always liked to remind them that this is a comedy," said Jensen. "People watch it because they want to laugh. Not to be preached to. I felt we always had to keep that in mind."

Jensen seemed to be wary of confrontation with both the show's message and real-life interaction. But he was widely trusted by nearly everyone in the production and seemed to get along especially well with Smith. And Will loved the special episodes.

His jokes, comebacks, and quips were rapid-fire and could carry any episode. But by the fourth season he wanted desperately to shed the label of being the prat who dazzled with charisma and physical comedy. He let it be known he was serious about acting. Winifred Hervey knew this. It had led to her exit.

His experience on the set of *Six Degrees of Separation* had changed him. He took acting lessons every weekend. He took endless meetings about starring in movies, too. He and James Lassiter had a specific plan. There was no turning back.

An Offer He Could Refuse

Shepard would finish Season Four on a satisfying note by snagging another writing credit on an episode titled "You

Better Shop Around" (Season Four, Episode 19). Will gets a job as a used car salesman and has to choose between the new well-paying gig or his education.

"We played that strictly for the laughs," said Shepard. "Nothing but funny shit."

It was gravy that it guest-starred legendary actor Robert Guillaume. Shepard had grown up a fan of hits like *Soap* and *Benson*, which made the actor a star. Those shows inspired him to become a writer. He had told Rob Edwards that in the barbershop when they first met.

"Here I am now with Robert Guillaume saying my words," said Shepard. "That was pretty cool."

After the final episode wrapped, the network quickly began staff exit interviews to shore up the production for Season Five. Showrunner Gary H. Miller asked Shepard to come to his office to discuss the future. Shepard was optimistic and felt he had done solid work despite the early bumps in the road. And that was despite the fact that he and Miller never really saw eye to eye that a deal could be worked out.

He was sure Miller would put forth an acceptable offer. He couldn't have been more wrong.

After going over the exceptional quality of his work, Miller landed a bombshell.

Shepard recalls Miller saying he had a "prejudice about where people come from and when you walk around here looking mean it intimidates everybody. You make people uncomfortable."

Shepard sat speechless. His blood was beginning to boil.

He thought about the confrontations. He thought about his lunch with Bill Boulware and how his pep talk began a transformation from within.

"If you come back next season," continued Miller, "I want you to smile more. It will make people more comfortable. Just smile."

A beat, then another. Boulware's speech had dissolved like ash in the wind.

"You can eat a fat baby's dick," said Shepard. With that he got up and left the room.

The kid from South Central had quit a hit network show, but this wasn't the end.

Shepard went on to work on several Black sitcoms, including *Everybody Hates Chris*, *The Wayans Bros.*, and *All About the Andersons*. Places, successful places, that didn't demand he change himself so completely for the comfort of his employers.

He never spoke to Gary Miller again.

"How Come He Don't Want Me?"

Ben Vereen woke up as if it were any other day. He was excited about an audition on Broadway the following week. He was up for the lead, you see. Those moments for a career actor are as sweet as they are elusive. He could make people smile with that voice of his and those eager dancing feet. He could do Fosse like no other, they all would say. If nothing else, he always had that.

Vereen was an accomplished character actor with a wide smile and engaging charm, who ping-ponged back and forth between television and the stage. His raspy baritone, quick wit, and ever-present smile made him a favorite among theatergoers and casting directors alike.

In 1977, Vereen reached the pinnacle of his career as Chicken George, an affable bird fighting handler in the acclaimed eight-part TV miniseries *Roots*. Based on the novel by Alex Haley, *Roots* was a critical and ratings smash that shot a generation of Black actors to new heights of public notoriety, including John Amos, LeVar Burton, and Cicely Tyson. Vereen would be nominated for two Primetime Emmys for his work, to go with the Tony he scooped up for the musical *Pippin*.

In the years after *Roots*, Vereen would land himself television roles in places like *The Love Boat* and *Webster* but never stray too far from the bright lights of Broadway. At age forty, though, his star began to fade and he could never equal the success of *Roots*, which was now a dozen years in the rearview mirror and a generation removed from public consciousness.

So much had changed around Vereen. Demographics and tastes had shifted. Hip-hop had exploded onto the scene in the prior decade and advertisers courted Gen Xers who were plugged into MTV. By 1992, Vereen was just another working actor whom no one could quite place. His career began to languish and Vereen felt unbalanced as an artist.

His manager routinely put out queries on his behalf to get him auditions. Vereen was trying to get a handle on where he wanted his career to go. Well, he knew the desired direction—up—but the means of conveyance he did not know. He was relatively young and still felt he had a lot to give.

In the early morning hours of June 9, 1992, Vereen was involved in a one-car accident not far from his Point Dume apartment in Malibu. He suffered a concussion, followed quickly by a small stroke after his prized Corvette Stingray left the roadway and struck a tree. Left dazed by the collision, Vereen found himself wandering along, hugging the Pacific Coast Highway's path beside the Southern California coast after being released from a sheriff's station.

He stumbled onto the median, then tried to right himself before stepping out into traffic again.

Across town, Canadian music producer David Foster was making his way home from a late-night studio session in Hollywood, where he had been recording with Michael Bolton. After leaving just after 2 a.m., he began the twenty-five-minute drive west to his home in Malibu.

At the corner of Sycamore Canyon and PCH, after cresting a hill in the night fog, Foster saw a shadowy figure in the middle of the road. He struck Vereen with his Chevrolet Suburban, sending his body flying thirty feet. Foster called 911.

"I think I just killed someone," he told the 911 operator.

Vereen was badly injured and lay on the cold, unforgiving pavement in a fetal position; blood pouring from his ears, nose, and mouth.

"I just destroyed his body," Foster recalled in his 2021 documentary about his life, *David Foster: Off the Record*.

"I'll tell you that the night that I hit Ben Vereen, that night and the next day or two after that were the worst days of my life. It was absolutely the worst," Foster told Yahoo! in 2020. "I never believed in flashbacks until that happened. And for three days, every 20 seconds or 30 seconds, I had it burning in my brain. It was insane."

Ironically, the disastrous circumstance provided Vereen with a stroke of lifesaving luck. As a result of the accidents,

237

doctors at UCLA Medical Center discovered his brain was bleeding and he would have likely died by dawn as a result of a subdural hematoma. He underwent four and a half hours of surgery on fractures, internal injuries, and swelling of the brain.

Vereen's recovery was long and arduous. He required years of painful rehabilitation and dozens of surgeries. Doctors told him that due to his shattered left leg, it would be years before he learned to walk again, if ever.

"I was pretty banged up," the now-seventy-four-year-old Vereen recalled to me. "I didn't know if I was going to walk again. My left leg was broken and the stroke paralyzed my right side. I had my spleen removed and was fitted with a colostomy bag. I was a very sick puppy.

"I mean, I was a dancer. Would I ever be able to do that again? I had just gone through an enormous amount of trauma and was grappling with my place in the universe when I heard a voice . . . and it was Will's.

"I would hear him in my dreams, when I meditated, when I struggled. . . . Will's voice was calling me."

"That's My Dad"

The Fresh Prince was in the middle of its fourth season and Will Smith was eager to test his thespian limits anew. The show had used fatherhood as a strong thread throughout its run but Will was usually a cursory player in those episodes.

He wanted to address fatherhood head-on and began

kicking ideas around about the Will character reuniting with his father, who had scarcely received a mention in the show's previous seasons. "Papa's Got a Brand New Excuse" (Season Four, Episode 24) would see Will's father Lou Smith's surprise return into his life after fourteen years.

The aim of the show was threefold: Uncle Phil would hit the height of his protective fatherly tendencies, it would shine a light on the importance of Black fatherhood, and Will could take a step he had long desired—flex his acting muscles as the centerpiece of a weighty story line.

Will considered himself a student of Black popular culture, soaking up everything from the Harlem Renaissance to Motown to the origins of hip-hop. It was he who suggested Ben Vereen for the role of the Fresh Prince's father. He had devoured *Roots* when it first aired and again in adulthood. There was even a Vereen reference in the first season. Arrangements were soon made and Vereen was on his way to Los Angeles to tape the episode.

"The first time I met Will was at the table read and he was so gracious," remembered Vereen. "The cast was warm and beautiful. But Will was like an ember that just burned so bright."

The episode begins with a hesitant Will reluctantly letting his father, Lou, back in his life. But their bond quickly builds and Will's heart soars. At an amusement park Lou tells him he was an all-city point guard back in Philly. He hits several shots to win a prize as a young boy looks on.

"He's pretty good," says the boy.

"That's my dad," beams Will.

It is the first time in his life he has ever said those words. Will is now completely invested in building a life with his father.

In the penultimate scene, after spending the week getting to know Lou, Will prepares to depart with him on a cross-country road trip back east. It is Lou's biggest job yet as a long-haul trucker. After an intense back-and-forth with Uncle Phil in the family room, the show perilously wades into uncharted dramatic waters. The audience, hushed, felt the weight of the moment. There would be no gags to puncture the solemn veneer.

"Tell Will I'll call him from the road," says Lou.

"I not gonna do your dirty work for you," counters Uncle Phil.

Will comes bounding in from the kitchen clutching his packed bag, buoyant about their adventure.

"Uh, Will, I'm glad you're here," says Lou. "Something came up."

Lou is unable to take Will because he needs an extra driver to help him make the distance in allotted time. Will is crestfallen. His new world is shattered in a moment.

"It was nice seeing you, son," says Lou, backing away.

"You, too . . . Lou."

Lou exits. Will is crushed. His defenses kick in.

"This actually works out better for me," he says with a wavering, unconvincing cool. "I heard the slimmies be coming to class with next to nothing on."

Uncle Phil looks at Will with sad compassion. Offers a life raft.

"Will, it's all right to be angry," he soothes.

Will's words pour out in a jumble of confusion and anger and hurt.

"Why should I be mad? At least he said good-bye this time. I just wish I hadn't wasted my money buying this stupid present. Hey, you know what, ain't like I'm still five years old, you know? Ain't like I'm going to be sitting up every night, asking my mom, 'When's Daddy coming home?' You know? Who needs him? Hey, he wasn't there to teach me how to shoot my first basket, but I learned, didn't I? And I got pretty damn good at it, too, didn't I, Uncle Phil? Got through my first date without him. I learned how to drive, I learned how to shave, I learned how to fight without him. I had fourteen great birthdays without him! He never even sent me a damn card.

"TO HELL WITH HIM!!"

It is a chilling moment that stuns both Avery and the audience.

Fade out.

"Breathe . . ."

Vereen stood off stage right and tried to settle himself. He exhaled and put his right hand temporarily over his heart. He let out another slow breath. His eyes were closed.

He pulled his character's black knit hat off his head. It

would remain in the closet of his Manhattan apartment for the next twenty-five years.

Will and James were standing not twenty-five feet away, engaged in what would be the series' most memorable moment.

"Breathe, breathe, breathe," Vereen mouthed to himself as he watched Smith and Avery.

Vereen was an actor. He cheered for actors. He wanted to see good acting. He was struck dumb by what happened next.

"I ain't need him then and I don't need him now!" insists Will.

"No, you know what, Uncle Phil? I'm gonna get through college without him, I'm gonna get me a great job without him, I'm gonna marry me a beautiful honey, I'm gonna have me a whole bunch of kids, and be a better father than he ever was. And I sure as hell don't need him for that, because there ain't a damn thing he could ever teach me about how to love my kids!"

An excruciating beat.

Will's anger begins to dissipate. He chokes up. He is without defense. Tears stream down his face. He is five years old again.

"What if?"

The episode's writer, Bill Boulware, had been ruminating on the idea for the show for quite some time. Years, in fact. When he was growing up, his parents divorced when Boulware was very young, and he was left with a feeling of emptiness. Now that his father was no longer in his life, his direction and drive began to wane.

"Fatherhood is a topic that I've always had an interest in from the perspective of both the father and the son," said Boulware. "When my parents split I wasn't allowed to see my dad but I really wanted to have a relationship with him. So the idea had been percolating in my mind for a while."

Boulware grew up in the impoverished Colonial Projects in Harlem, right next to the famed Polo Grounds. He could look out his window and see center field at the Bathtub, where the New York Giants played. In the eighth grade his mother enrolled him in the small but predominately Jewish New Lincoln School, on 110th Street in Harlem. There he began to fall in love with books and writing. He would devour the work of novelists Graham Greene and Jack London and excel at writing dramatic short stories.

He gave up his dream of becoming a writer after completing his undergraduate degree at Wesleyan University. Fresh into the real world, he found little encouragement and support for his ambition. He instead took a job at Syracuse University as an admissions officer in charge of recruiting minority students, while earning his master's in city planning.

He kept busy, but it wasn't where he wanted to be and he wasn't taking much home at the end of the day, either. He was disillusioned and broke, but the writer's dream stayed alight within him the whole time. On a whim, the young

Boulware applied to film school at Boston University. Even crazier, he got in. Upon graduation in 1977, he was accepted to a writing program at Columbia Pictures in Los Angeles, which launched his screenwriting career. After stints on *Benson* and *The White Shadow*, he created the hit Black family sitcom *227*, which ran for five years and turned out 115 episodes.

Immediately after *227* ended he got wind of a new pilot starring the inexperienced rapper-turned-actor who went by the name the Fresh Prince. After a round of interviews, Boulware was told indirectly that he was too old for the show. That he was out of touch with street culture. His lack of hip-hop knowledge didn't help.

"Basically," Boulware lamented, "I wasn't hip enough. Then I watched the show and thought, *You think I couldn't write that?*"

But the opportunity would come back around with Season Four of *The Fresh Prince* as Boulware was hired as a supervising producer (by Gary H. Miller, the least hip executive ever associated with the show).

At thirty-nine, the wounds from his father's absence were still raw.

"My dad had let me down so many times," Boulware explained, "but no matter how many times it happened I still wanted him in my life. I wanted Will to go through the same thing."

Boulware's mother felt that his father, who had dropped out of high school, had not played a big enough role in his life and did not deserve to see his son. He wasn't the kind of person he needed to be around, reasoned his mother.

While the show's producers had passed over him four years earlier, he regularly watched the show, mostly to support his friend and showrunner, Winifred Hervey, one of the few Black female executives in Hollywood. Boulware was struck by the fact that Will's father was almost completely absent from the show without any real explanation. The fact was highlighted by the constant recurring presence of Will's mother, Vy, who had made appearances in every season.

Given his personal experience, Boulware saw an opening.

"Each show starts off with a 'what if,'" said Boulware. "So in that week's pitch meeting I said, 'What if Will's father comes back in his life?'"

Since the subject matter was heavier fare than normal, Boulware teamed up with staff writer David Zuckerman as the clock ticked toward showtime. Often when writers on the show would team up, each would take a turn hammering out the script and hand it back to his partner until they had a finished product to send to the showrunner. But on "Papa's Got a Brand New Excuse," they locked themselves in a room and wrote together from page one.

The pair knocked the script up in about two days before sending it over to showrunner Gary H. Miller, who returned it with few notes. Miller told Will they had something special from the start and the actor lit up after reading the script. It had been exactly what he was looking for.

But there was one thing that stood out to Smith more than anything else: the monologue at the end of the show. They were words not unlike the kind he'd always wanted to say to his own father. Will's had not abandoned him like his fictional counterpart's had, but he had left a wound with his overbearing, unemotional parenting. These were feelings Will had held forever, but even more so now—what the audience and writers hadn't known, couldn't have known, is that Will Smith, the actor, had become a father himself. His first son, Trey, was born to his first wife, Sheree Zampino, eighteen months earlier, during Season Three of *The Fresh Prince*. Smith's 1997 hit "Just the Two of Us" is an ode to Trey and explores how fatherhood transformed him.

"How come he don't want me, man?"

Avery, instinctually parental, pulls him close. Will buries his head in his chest. Never more has he been his son.

Until that moment, Avery, a master craftsman, knew to keep his distance. He knew that Will Smith, the actor, was being born in that moment. He knew how much Will chased the evolution of his own acting ability. Will would spend hours in Avery's dressing room picking his brain on every branch of the arts. He was obsessed with process. He hated to make mistakes. He wanted to make Avery proud.

It was part of Smith's deep-seated desire to please, which was born out of the complexities of his relationship with his own father. He admired his father but had also witnessed him strike his mother, a fact he would not speak about for forty-four years.

"An Actor is Born"

Avery was known for his exceptional patience as an actor. Equal parts forgiving and encouraging, he could keep his distance or engage. He could incite or disarm. He was a force. His talent was equaled only by his imposing stature. But Avery knew a moment when he saw one.

The script had called for the very words Smith spoke. But Avery knew Smith had plumbed unexpected depths. He had grown quiet in the days leading up to the taping. He had avoided Avery. This was not an anomaly. Smith would find quiet moments in alcoves or the conference room at the end of the hallway.

He would disappear both from the world and into his character. He wouldn't talk to anyone. He would pace. Agonize. Second-guess. Frustration bubbled over into fits of passion and doubt.

Avery was startled by Will's performance despite several table reads and rehearsals. He'd also always known he had it in him. So did Vereen, tears streaming down his face in the aftermath of Will's monologue.

Will Smith, the man, had entered stage left and exited a different actor.

"That wasn't acting," said Vereen. "That was being. That was real. It was an incredible moment."

The studio audience, who had been so conditioned to laugh, was silent. Sniffles could be heard under the original taping. A woman gasped. The episode had ended not to the typical buoyant soundtrack, but to an appropriate silence instead.

For all their ambition and promise and naiveté born from a need to fit in, the cast, a once-ragtag group of new-comers, stage veterans, and a rapper, together four years this winter, could not have known their collective efforts could reach such emotional heights and lay bare the deepest parts of their being.

They wept.

Hitting Their Stride

It was time for a little fun. In the spring of 1994, the fourth season of *The Fresh Prince of Bel-Air* had just wrapped and was arguably the production's best yet. Karyn Parsons and her friends met up with frequent *Fresh Prince* director Shelley Jensen in Las Vegas, determined to get fully into the spirit of the Sin City. They hatched a plan to toss their underwear onstage, as women were frequently known to do, at a Tom Jones show that weekend. They purchased cheap ladies' drawers at the gift shop at Caesars Palace to prepare. Shortly before the concert they were joined by Alfonso Ribeiro and his friends, who were returning from a prizefight.

"It was a fun idea but when it came time to execute it we kinda botched it," said Parsons. "We just couldn't find the right moment to run to the stage. Everyone was seated so it felt awkward. We threw them at the last moment as the curtain was coming down. It didn't exactly work."

Ribeiro got into the spirit and delighted fans from his seat, performing the Carlton Dance as Jones belted out "It's Not Unusual." Afterward the group headed backstage.

"Me being naïve, I ran up to Tom and told him about our panty-tossing escapade," Parsons remembered. Jones stepped right up to Parsons and looked her up and down. "I just shrunk," she said with a laugh.

"I was mortified!"

"As a person they don't come finer than Karyn," laughed Jensen, "but it was damn funny."

"We All We Got"

Back home in Los Angeles, their lives were changing in ways they had always dreamed about but could never imagine. Will was on magazine covers. Ribeiro was a regular on the talk show circuit and began getting besieged by fan requests to do the Carlton Dance.

But to Parsons things still felt normal.

"My life really didn't change much over the course of the show," she said. Not at least until it was in syndication. "They would usher me to the front of the line at the club but that was about it.

"When we first started the show, the first thing Will told

us was that we wouldn't be able to go to the mall anymore. That didn't happen for me. It wasn't until we stopped shooting until people started to approach.

"I don't generally look like Hilary when I go out. I don't wear makeup. I'm not decked out in Chanel suits. But occasionally people always say, 'You look like the girl on *The Fresh Prince.*'"

But getting fan mail—back when people actually wrote letters—was a new and welcome experience. Even though most of the mail was from prison. "They were generally very nice," she said, "but occasionally you get someone with a foot fetish."

Still the cast, the human beings at the center of this all-consuming machine, tried to close ranks and bond more than ever. In fact, Parsons moved from the Park La Brea apartments to the Valley to be closer to her castmates in Glendale.

As Parsons's paychecks steadily grew—and she was now adept at balancing her checkbook—she decided it was time to buy her first home. She settled on a Spanish Revival on Floyd Terrace, just off the 101, to be closer to NBC Studios in Glendale. At just twenty-two years old, it was the first time she had ever lived in a house after being raised in multiple apartments in Santa Monica. She loved the hardwood floors, soaring arches, and abundance of sunlight. The two working fireplaces and meditation room she decorated with pillows and rugs made her feel so at ease when she returned home from work.

On Saturdays Parsons would get a standing massage ("I

carried so much tension in my back!") followed by a hot bath or some relaxing meditation time that would both take her mind off the previous week and get her loose for the upcoming one.

She would meet up with her friends for brunches or quick shopping excursions.

"Hilary crap," she said, "even though I didn't think I was Hilary."

She was initially inspired to move to Glendale by the fact that Alfonso Ribeiro had found a place a few blocks over in the hilly neighborhood, after going to dinners at his house.

"I just wanted to be close to him," she remembered. "I wanted to be close to my brother."

They would often carpool to work, singing along with the radio, sometimes eighties hits or R&B. At work one afternoon the cast was walking through a courtroom scene, setting the blocking, when in a moment of boredom Parsons playfully slapped Alfonso's face. Will's eyes went wide.

"Oh no she didn't!" shouted Will. "You gonna let her slap you like that?"

The gears in Ribeiro's head began turning. A devilish look came across his face.

"Don't you do it!" warned Parsons.

Slap!

Ribeiro returned the favor. Will broke up. It was soft and playful. All in fun. But Parsons would have the last word. When the actors were told to go home at the end of the day, Alf went out into the parking lot.

"Hey, where's Karyn?" said a quizzical Ribeiro. "She's my ride home!"

For Parsons the silly moments were as valuable as the real. But her castmates would be there when it hurt the most.

One of the cast and crew's most challenging moments during the show's six-year run came in the final season on the first Tuesday in October. And it had nothing to do with characters, conflicts, or punch lines. The cast and writers had just sat down for the first table read of the week. There was a large-screen monitor in the room, which was tuned to the O. J. Simpson verdict.

In the penultimate moment there was a split screen. On the right were predominately white college students; the left was a Black barbershop. The table read for the episode "Bourgie Sings the Blues" (Season Six, Episode 4) was complete. Before the verdict was read, the writers, who were mostly white, begin slinking out of the room and up to their writers' cave.

The all-Black cast remained downstairs.

"We were separated," said Parsons. "That was not lost on me."

The separation both on-screen and among the crew bothered Parsons and made her uncomfortable.

"I was mortified and devastated," said Parsons. "People were cheering because they thought the system had worked for a Black man and I thought a murderer got off. It just felt like everyone was being pitted against one another. It hurt so bad. It was just so painful to me."

She went to her dressing room and began to cry. One

by one her castmates entered her room. First Tatyana. Then
Alfonso. Lastly Will. They began to hug and console her.
Will tried to explain how he felt. They all expressed their
thoughts on what had just transpired.

They were not actors on a hit show in that moment.
They weren't colleagues. They had been exactly what they
were to each other the last six years.

Siblings.

"Jumping the Shark"

In the summer before the sixth season of *The Fresh Prince of
Bel-Air,* Smith was seemingly hitting all of his show business
and personal goals.

His summer action follow-up to 1995's *Bad Boys,* the
alien invasion epic *Independence Day,* was a Goliath hit, gross-
ing $817 million, making it the highest-grossing movie of
1996 and beginning Smith's meteoric run as the most bank-
able star in Hollywood.

Now commanding $20 million a picture, Smith had the
kind of options he'd never had before. He knew *The Fresh
Prince* wasn't going to run forever. And despite the fact that
the ratings had dipped slightly, it remained one of prime
time's most popular comedies. The network was pleased and
wanted to keep it going several more years. The cast loved
the work and the fact that they had secure jobs. A *Fresh Prince*
credit looked great on a writer's resume, too.

It seemed everyone was happy.

Except Will.

After the fifth season he felt the show was growing stale and "hokey" and that it was becoming increasingly harder to match the quality of previous seasons. The tipping point—when Will felt the show jumped the shark—was a dramatic special episode titled "Bullets over Bel-Air" (Season Five, Episode 15), where Will is shot in a robbery and Carlton begins carrying a gun. The episode was well received by the network and remains a favorite of viewers.

It ranks as the fourth-best *Fresh Prince* episode via fan voting on IMDb. Television website Decider ranks it as the fifth, while another, TV Insider, slots it at No. 9.

It was one of *The Fresh Prince*'s beloved special episodes, where a dramatic story line would take precedence and the characters would grow and change in some profound way. "Papa's Got a Brand New Excuse" (Season Four, Episode 24) and "Blood Is Thicker than Mud" (Season Four, Episode 17) are examples done to near perfection and are the very best of what the show could accomplish.

But to Will, "Bullets Over Bel-Air" didn't work. It felt forced, as if the show was trying to create a moment. He had had issues with special episodes before, but Will wasn't so much in the fighting mood this time around. He was a movie star and already had his parachute on.

In fact, there is considerable debate on whether the fifth season almost didn't happen. A long-held rumor is that NBC wanted to cancel the show after the fourth season—arguably its best—due to lagging but still acceptable ratings. *The Fresh Prince*'s fan base caught wind of the chatter and protested, in the form of an avalanche of fan mail and letters to the network. NBC's president, Warren Littlefield, and his programming executives reversed course and renewed the show for a fifth season.

No producers or executives contacted could remember such a scenario. As detailed in previous chapters, the cast and crew themselves rarely ever knew when a show would be canceled, let alone did a pre-internet fanbase. Even in the plugged-in era of smartphones, endless entertainment websites, social media, and streaming services, news of a show's cancellation today almost always comes as a surprise to fans.

While cast members of *The Fresh Prince* did receive large quantities of fan mail, it often took months for the actors to read them and they would have played no role in whether or not NBC renewed. Executives focused on one thing—ratings—which determined advertising rates and were the standard for whether or not a show lived or died.

Good shows get canceled all the time if they don't perform well. *The Fresh Prince*'s ratings had lagged but were respectable enough for NBC to continue production. (They would make it to Season Six and likely would have filmed a seventh if Smith had not left to pursue a movie career.)

But reaching in the dark to keep the show fresh had grown tiresome for Will.

Above all, he wanted to be a movie star. That had been the plan since the day he and his manager, James Lassiter, broke down the reasons why the top ten movies of all time were successful—special effects, aliens, love stories—and used their findings as a blueprint to make Will the biggest star in the world. He was relentless in pursuit of that goal.

Will would often skip the cast lunches, instead taking business lunches in the office with Lassiter and prospective collaborators. They met with producers and directors and pored over scripts.

Near the end, when people could sense it was not far from over, they began to bond all that much more. They weren't as quick to leave when work was over. As if instinctively savoring the moments. Most nights after the show, Jensen and the actors would retreat to the upstairs conference room and play poker for hours. As he tells it, Jensen would usually make off with the lion's share of the winnings.

Knowing that *The Fresh Prince* wouldn't last forever, Parsons began to get aggressive with regard to auditioning. The show taped in the winter, so the cast's ability to go out for projects was a small window in the summer. She would go out for what seemed like a new project every week, reminding her of her pre–*Fresh Prince* grind.

Parsons auditioned for the Damon Wayans movie *Blankman* but just missed out on getting the part. (Robin Givens got it.) Wayans and his producers were, however, impressed and brought her back in to read for *Major Payne*, which she did get.

But on auditions she found herself running into a consistent roadblock: Halle Berry.

"Halle just got everything. She was just snatching up projects like dandelions in a field."

All Good Things

With each passing episode of Season Six there was an ever-increasing feeling of finality. Time seemed to speed up and blend the days, weeks, and hours together. The cast members' emotions would bubble with each curtain call or whenever they removed their makeup. They seemed to be hugging all the time.

The writers had been working for months on how the Banks family would say good-bye and decided they would say good-bye to Bel-Air altogether.

The Bankses had flirted with leaving their beloved Bel-Air enclave before, in "For Sale by Owner" (Season Four, Episode 25). Looking back, the episode created one of the most bizarre moments in *Fresh Prince* history. A mysterious bidder has made a cash offer of $1 million above market value because he had lived in the house in the 1950s and wants to buy it back for sentimental reasons.

In the last act the buyer arrives. Geoffrey answers the door.

"It is my esteemed pleasure to introduce Mr. and Mrs. Donald Trump," Geoffrey announces to the family.

Upon sighting Trump, noted Republican Carlton faints.

"You look much richer in person," says a giddy Hilary.

The only family member who's not on board is Ashley, who had been born in the house at 805 St. Cloud Road and is strongly opposed to its sale. In a huff, she steps up to Trump and in an eerily prophetic way tells him what she thinks.

"Thank you for ruining my life!" screams Ashley before storming off.

"Everybody's always blaming me for everything," replies Trump, tapping a briefcase full of cash.

The forty-seven-year-old real estate mogul wasn't exactly a hit with the cast and crew. Daphne Maxwell Reid refused to shake his hand after hearing stories about him in New York. Frustrated by real estate details in the story, Trump tossed his script on the ground.

"With all due respect," said showrunner Gary H. Miller, "I would never think of giving you any advice about real estate because I don't know about real estate. But I do know comedy and trust me, you'll get a laugh."

(Trump still makes a couple hundred dollars a year from his *Fresh Prince* cameo.)

"I really don't have a huge recollection of it, thank God,"

said Parsons. "I wasn't really impressed or excited. It wasn't like Zsa Zsa Gabor was coming."

The last two episodes of the series focus on the Bankses splitting up and actually leaving Bel-Air for good this time.

In "I Done" (Season Six, Episodes 23 and 24), the Bankses are selling the house for good this time. They're heading off to different parts of the country and separating for the first time in their lives. Carlton is off to Princeton to study law. Hilary will be heading to New York to host her own talk show, while Ashley will be both her producer and roommate while attending NYU. Geoffrey is packing his bags to move back to England to be with his son. Uncle Phil and Aunt Viv are downsizing and moving to a new neighborhood, where Nicky will start kindergarten.

Will's plans are as uncertain as the day he arrived.

"Well, looks like we're all in the fast lane except Will," jibes Carlton. "Someone has to be stuck on the soft shoulder."

In one final, glorious scheme, Will hatches a plan to discourage prospective buyers from making an offer on the house. He successfully gets rid of Conrad Bain and Gary Coleman (*Diff'rent Strokes*), Sherman Hemsley, Isabel Sanford, and Marla Gibbs (*The Jeffersons*) with stories about Indian burial grounds and topless Memorial Day pool parties next door.

The Jeffersons end up buying the house.

"Something about Memorial Day," says a bemused Uncle Phil.

(In one last sign of this unlikely phenomenon's luck,

in the final episode Will sports Air Jordan 11s and Nike Air Penny sneakers. On the exact day and time the episode aired, the Chicago Bulls played the Orlando Magic in the 1996 NBA playoffs, where Michael Jordan and Penny Hardaway faced off in the same shoes.)

The family is leaving home in a week. But Will is the only one whose next step isn't quite set. He still has to finish school. He doesn't have a job waiting for him. He doesn't have a place to live yet. He's been lying to Uncle Phil in one last effort to prove he can do it on his own. After the sale to the Jeffersons he confesses to his uncle about his plight.

Despite the progress he's made as a man, what he's learned, how he's grown, he feels like the directionless kid who first arrived on the doorstep of a new life.

"Why did you lie?" asks Uncle Phil sternly.

"I didn't want you to think that all these years out here just ain't been worth nothing," says Will. "That you've just been wasting your time with me. I just don't want you to think that I'm that same stupid kid I was when I first moved out here."

Uncle Phil gives that paternal look that has soothed Will many times over. He needs it now more than ever.

"How could you possibly believe that's what I'd be thinking?" he replies. "Look at you. You're becoming a man . . . A man I'm damn proud of."

He stares down at the ground. Will is seventeen again.

"I just didn't want your last memory to be no better than the first one."

"You have no idea what my first memory of you is," Uncle Phil says gently. "I remember a kid loaded with all the potential in the world. Who is a man on the verge of realizing that potential."

They embrace.

So Hard to Say Good-bye

After the final emotional table read earlier that day, the room fell silent. Scripts and pencils were strewn about the twenty-foot-long table. Coffee cups here and there. Producers on one side. The actors on the other.

Will sat in a speckled white hoodie and his hat turned backward. He was strangely quiet and withdrawn. He had made the yet-to-be-released *Independence Day* the previous summer. The bold and unafraid conqueror of an alien invasion who would save the world.

But here he looked like he was back at Overbrook High on the first day of school. Not knowing what would happen.

Hopeful and scared. Mostly both.

His brother Alfonso was to his left.

Will and Carlton's relationship had come the furthest. Solidified through a real love, respect, and admiration, it was at its conclusion. At that table they read through the last scene they would ever do together.

Will and Carlton are in the pool house, packing their belongings. Will wears a Negro League Pittsburgh Crawfords sweatshirt, Carlton a Polo sweater. "It's been a good trip," Carlton says to Will, their bags slowly filling.

"It's been a great trip. Look, whenever, wherever . . . I got your back, C."

The poignant moment of brotherhood closes, as always with a laugh, as the final credits near and Will puts a CD in the stereo. "You got to do it one last time for me."

Tom Jones plays as Will and Carlton do the Carlton Dance.

In the studio, Joseph Marcell removed his glasses and dabbed his eyes with a tissue. Seeing the unflappable Geoffrey cry was more than most in the room could handle.

Next to him was Karyn Parsons. "We're such a family now," she said, "and it's so sad . . . this is so hard."

James Avery consoled her by touching her on the shoulder.

Through choked voices and sad eyes, they would read their last script. People nervously cleared their throats if only to buy a moment to steady themselves. To hold emotions at bay.

Then Avery spoke.

"This has been very unique for all of us," he said to rapt attention, "and I can honestly say, because I've been working for fifteen years, that this is the best experience, in terms of people and friends and happiness. . . ."

Avery stopped himself without finishing the thought. He welled up.

Later that night on the set, Will Smith picked up the microphone and ascended the steps into the arms of the anxiously awaiting crowd whom he had moved 147 times before. This would be the last time he would ever do this. He wore a white T-shirt tucked into yellow sweatpants and black-and-white Fila high-tops.

His voice cracked. He hesitated.

"Y'all know that this the final episode of *Fresh Prince of Bel-Air*, right?" he said, trying to sound tough and unwavering. Failing thoroughly. "You know it's sad but we had a six-year run . . . so we would like you to sit back . . . and enjoy . . . *The Fresh Prince of Bel-Air* comin' at ya for the last time!"

He left the stands and walked back down to the floor. Some said he looked disoriented, flustered, ruffled. He held back tears.

As he would many times this night.

"You Are My Son"

With all the furniture removed, Will Smith and James Avery's Uncle Phil meet in the empty living room, on the rug, for *The Fresh Prince of Bel-Air*'s final scene.

"When I moved out here I was a relative," says Will, "but for the past six years we been family. I want you to call me on Sundays like you call your other kids. I just don't want to lose you."

"You are my son, Will," says Uncle Phil in the show's most profound moment. "You just better be sure that your butt is by a phone on Sundays."

This is the moment that the series comes full circle. After 148 episodes. Six seasons. Fights, arguments, tears. Lessons learned and taught. A boy who became a man. An uncle who became a father. They could not do this without each other.

In the first episode of *The Fresh Prince of Bel-Air*, Uncle Phil disowns Will before he can get to know him. He stresses to Vivian that Will is his nephew by marriage only.

And in this moment Uncle Phil is staring at his son. With whom he cannot do without.

The first time James Avery met Will Smith, he told him to get his feet off the table.

Will was his son from that moment forward.

They hug.

Uncle Phil leaves for the kitchen.

Geoffrey enters.

"Good-bye, Master William," says Geoffrey.

"Bye, G," says Will sadly.

An excruciating beat.

"Good-bye . . . Will."

They embrace. It is the first and only time in the series that Geoffrey would call him Will.

As Geoffrey leaves, Uncle Phil reenters.

Uncle Phil turns to leave. Stops. He points at Will.

"Sunday," he says before leaving Will's life.

It is profound. It is full circle. It is the embodiment and completion of Uncle Phil.

Remembered director Shelley Jensen:

That was a tough episode because it was an era ending. I staged it where he turns the lights out and the camera pulls back. It makes me emotional just thinking about it. We were all thinking whether or not we were going to see something like this again in our careers. And the answer was no. This was as good as it gets.

But Smith had his sights set. He recalled to the *Los Angeles Times* in 1996, the day after the show ended:

You become a family. On some weeks you spend more time with your TV family than you do with your real family. It's hard to say goodbye to that atmosphere, but we felt like it was time. We've all grown as actors and as people, we had an incredibly talented cast, but the show is just limiting.

TV is a good workout facility, where you get to work on your timing and other paces, but I think I've had enough time in the gym. Now I'm ready for the coach to put me in the game . . . motion pictures.

"Turning Out the Lights"

Before the last act, the crew had to come out and remove all of the furniture and accoutrements in the Bankses' living room, which America had become so familiar with for so many years.

The couch. The chairs. The paintings. The foosball table. The vases. The sculptures. The fake set props.

Everything the Bankses never owned was gone in a flash, loaded onto a dolly and removed for the last time. It was wheeled offstage and out of consciousness.

There was only one item left. Something we had never noticed before but beckoned our attention because *our* living room had been stripped away. Not in six years had we noticed.

But there it remained.

The rug.

After the final scene with Will and Uncle Phil, Will stands on the rug in an otherwise empty room, wearing faded blue jeans and white-and-metallic-silver Air Jordan 11s. In the future it would become one of the internet's most popular memes.

But in this moment Will Smith from West Philadelphia, who was sent to live with his aunt Viv and uncle Phil, would look at this safe living room one last time.

So would the real Will Smith.

Both walked off the set for the last time. Both were crying.

Will walks into the kitchen and waits. He raises his hands to his eyes as the tears begin to pour. Helplessly wiping them away.

He has no more lines.

Here are Jensen's parting thoughts, through a cracked voice, on the final episode:

Sitcoms are a weird thing. It's like being a gypsy. You become really tight and all of a sudden the show is canceled because eventually they are all canceled. Then the family breaks up and then you go to your next family. But *Fresh Prince* was a much tighter family than most. There was an energy on that show that was unmatched by any show I've ever worked on. Oftentimes when you work with actors the last time you see them is when you say "cut" for the final time. We're all still friends to this day. Not a week goes by where I don't talk to someone I worked with on the show. We still play golf together. When we talk it's like we are still on the set. And we've been off the air for twenty-five years.

"The final week was interesting," said a reflective Smith on HBO Max's *Fresh Prince of Bel-Air Reunion*. "It was fuzzy in my mind. That's part of my emotional defense. I always live in the future. I think as a child that's how I learned to avoid the pain of a present moment.

"I see pictures from that week and it was such a painful good-bye."

And yet these are the moments you wait for all your life.

The audience filed out. The actors headed back to their dressing rooms to cry and hug some more. They were struck by the finality of seeing the furniture and props stacked on dollies. Jazzy Jeff left before the taping ended, as did some of the crew, unable to bear the long, sorrowful good-byes.

The set was already dark.

And just like that, it was over.

Will was the last one to leave.

EPILOGUE

Will Smith was fifty-two.

That family in Hawaii that he had dismantled as easily as it came together was staring directly at him. They were all far from Bel-Air as he held a toast, far better than he held his composure. These were people he had never met before he walked into Quincy Jones's living room.

This troupe had, after all, saved his life.

But this was different. He didn't want anyone to be blind-sided.

Will hated to let people down.

So no wine was wasted. No song unsung. No joke untold.

Laughs bellowed. Hearts swelled. Eyes welled.

Hawaii's skies would open up as they do. Plump, warm drops would splatter.

Laughter would echo. Memories would reverberate. Hugs felt permanent, even if they weren't.

Lessons and wounds. Healed and learned in equal capacity.

In the way Janet Hubert softly touched his face, with teary eyes, just as she had thirty-two years before, when Will would learn a lesson in the Bankses' family room.

Alfonso Ribeiro, who gave him the best advice anyone had—keep your name.

James Avery would pound his chest and tell him, "You're not a rapper here, but an actor . . ."

And he was right. And the kid listened. Because he wanted to learn. He wanted to earn every accolade.

He didn't want to let anyone down.

The boy from Woodcrest Avenue had spent six years trying to prove it. Trying to win his approval. Same as Daddio's. He was not exactly sure if he ever did. In either case. The first time he met Avery, the latter told him to get his feet off the table. If you didn't respect elders you didn't respect yourself.

Willard Carroll understood.

His grandmother Gigi told him the same before he could walk.

That's why James could pound his chest.

That's how Will became an actor.

That's how he became a man.

● ● ●

the hippie
the dancing kid from broadway
the dj from his mom's basement
the little girl who moved across country
that rapper guy who had no other option

272

the beauty from santa monica

the carpenter's son from england

They were strangers. Only until they weren't.

They came crashing into each other's lives and our living rooms and with equal efficacy. Their brand of bombast and silliness. Without warning.

More than thirty years ago. And landed safely.

And we have not yet asked them to leave.

● ● ●

The Fresh Prince of Bel-Air, this lark, this silly thing, with all its fluorescent pinks and yellows and greens, became emblazoned on our collective consciousness. With aplomb. With verve and ambition. And all those other words you're not supposed to say when you're cool. Think "Prince used a school word!" (Season One, Episode 23, "72 Hours." RIP Tiny "Zeus" Lister.)

Yet we offered no contestation. Not so much as a half-hearted rebuttal.

There was none to give.

We laughed at its absurdity, its farce, its humor, only to be struck still by its maddening poignancy.

We wanted it to be real. And we still do.

We wanted Uncle Phil to be our father.

We saw ourselves in Carlton.

We wished we could date Hilary.

We marveled at Aunt Viv's grace.

We protected Ashley.

We wanted to *be* Will.

And we needed G's advice.

The show punctured our own falsehoods. It laid bare what we didn't want others to know about ourselves even though we knew they were experiencing the same.

We laughed.

If only to keep from crying.

But it's just a sitcom, right?

Yes, it is. And we tell sweet little lies about ourselves and those things that we see on TV that we want to be.

We smile. At all our friends.

We are thankful for the Banks family. They were just actors.

But their indomitable love for one another brought us to tears. To rubble. When, in fact, it was meant to build us up.

Maybe we only found the lessons in syndication. When we were older. Late at night on TBS.

We find safety in the Bankses' triumphs and a familiarity in their failures. We hate that they're gone, but love that they're still here.

But mostly we just wanted to laugh. That's why 8 p.m. on a Monday night was so important.

The Fresh Prince of Bel-Air was a mirror and a window.

A sitcom, right?

● ● ●

He can see Woodcrest. He can touch his father. He can hear her voice on the air. He can hug and he can cry. He can laugh the laugh they still say can be heard three houses away. He can feel the weight of her unchanging eyes.

There is so much beauty around him.

Will Smith. From West Philadelphia. Born and raised.

A fish out of water he remains. As we all do.

But the biggest fish in the river gets that way by never being caught.

ACKNOWLEDGMENTS

Joseph Marcell piloted the Jeep Cherokee down the 101 Freeway in Los Angeles, a mercilessly ragged concrete haphazard of a thoroughfare that is unavoidable on nearly any north Los Angeles excursion.

He and his best friend were headed to a dog park.

James Avery sat in the passenger seat while his two beloved Old English sheepdogs were safely tucked away in the back seat. Their eager, floppy ears pricked up because they knew the route. They knew that the beloved Shakespearean actor, the leviathan of kindness, wisdom, and dog food portions, had the thing coveted above all—tennis balls.

They would give their chase, full stride, on the open yards and return off-yellow Penn tennis balls that came three to a can. Without fail.

Marcell had appeared alongside his friend James in 146 episodes of *The Fresh Prince of Bel-Air*. The show had been off the air for eighteen years. Yet still they remained the best of friends.

Marcell always had a place to stay at Avery's with his wife, Barbara. He would often venture back to Los Angeles when he was on hiatus with the Royal Shakespeare Company, his true love, which he returned to after *The Fresh Prince* ended.

Marcell's fondness for Avery was indefatigable. He cared for the lug. His love for James could make him cry. Move him. He was never Uncle Phil to him. Or "sir."

He was the hippie he met in 1990, when they shared a smoke outside NBC in Burbank. They had bonded over Shakespearean monologues and August Wilson plays.

Neither had even met Will Smith yet.

Shit, they'd never heard of him.

Humanity, kindness, and empathy got to Marcell like that. He would bare his soul to those he loved. Actors are coy. But to each other, James and Joseph weren't actors.

They were friends.

James liked that Joe was kind and forgiving.

Joe loved his warmth, and that he wore his vulnerability as honor.

James wanted to take his dogs out. When Joe was in town he would go with him. So they went to the dog park that day.

A few days later, when Avery couldn't find his wits, seemed disoriented, and was taken to the hospital, Joe was there.

Marcell sat by Avery's bedside in the hospital before his wife arrived.

"I you love, dear friend," said Marcell, sensing his own mortality.

Avery, knowing this, asked for a final favor.

"Can you get me two Big Macs from McDonald's?" Avery asked. "Just sneak them in."

"I can't do that," Marcell replied. "I would get caught."

Avery laughed at the absurdity of his own request in his final hours.

He asked once again about his beautiful dogs.

James had the love of a dear friend from distant shores who reciprocated with a tidal force.

He wouldn't go to McDonald's that day but he would hold his hand.

Seven days later, on December 31, 2013, James Avery died due to complications from open heart surgery.

Upon hearing the news, Joseph Marcell, the carpenter's son, sat quietly alone, still, and cried.

● ● ●

Will Smith stood on the stage of the Dolby Theatre in Hollywood. His voice wavered and cracked. No, not that time. Five months prior. He was promoting his book, *Will*.

It was the twenty-ninth birthday of his firstborn son, Trey, who sat about ten rows from the stage next to his mother, Sheree, Will's first wife. Not far away was Benny Medina, the man whose idea started it all. Several rows over was Charlie Mack. He insisted Will talk to Medina that day thirty-two years before at *The Arsenio Hall Show*.

It was a three-minute conversation.

Jada smiled. So did his son Jaden. Willow was there, too.

From the stage Will looked at each of them and said, "Thank you."

In every way he was there because of them.

● ● ●

When I was young, *The Fresh Prince of Bel-Air* was one of the first shows I was allowed to watch. My mom, from Green Bay, Wisconsin, would watch it with me. I remember her laughing at Carlton and Will doing the Running Man.

We bonded over *The Fresh Prince*. We would go see *Independence Day* and *Men in Black* at the AMC 6. She loved Will Smith, for the reasons Brandon Tartikoff said people would. We watched a dashing young man—brash, brave, funny, vulnerable—who seemed to be preternaturally skilled at saving the world.

It's a small thing to bond over a movie or a character with someone you love. It's also everything.

We talked about Will in our Ford Taurus on the car ride home.

I called my mother recently and we laughed about early episodes of *The Fresh Prince*. The show meant many different things to so many. But that's what it meant to me.

● ● ●

I would like to give thanks to those who made this work possible.

First are my mother, Sally, who is a far better writer, and my father, Ransford, whom she met her sophomore year in

1965 at Marquette, by way of Jamaica, and who taught at Howard University for forty-five years. Both of them nurtured my dreams to write.

In addition, a huge shout-out to my agents, Marc Gerald and Tess Callero, for believing in me and guiding me through this entire process. Your invaluable efforts have made this possible.

I also gotta holla at teachers whose names I can't entirely remember. My ninth-grade English teacher at Central High School in Prince George's County, Maryland, was Ms. Arnold. I can still see those used, ratty textbooks opened to the chapter with subject-verb agreement. Underlined by generations past. To this day, when I get lost, I close my eyes and picture those pages.

Thank you to every teacher and guidance counselor who pushed me to pursue my writing dreams and helped me to develop a talent. Thank you to the editors I've had over the years who made me a better writer simply by saving me from myself.

To all of my friends from Maryland who ask me how the writing's going. I say "good" even when it isn't. Godfather. Babe. Sarita. Sierra. Andrew. Elizabeth. Gavo Jr. Factory Haynes. Mr. Hughes. KJ. Owen. Cree Fontaine. And of course, the Nation.

BIBLIOGRAPHY

Books

Armstrong, Jennifer; *Seinfeldia: How A Show About Nothing Changed Everything*, Simon & Schuster, 2016

Berenson, Jan; *Will Power! A Biography of Will Smith*, Simon Spotlight Entertainment, 1997

Green, Victor H.; *The Negro Motorist Green Book Compendium*, About Comics, 2019

Hubert, Janet; *Perfection Is Not A Sitcom Mom*, self-published, 2008

Iannucci-Brinkley, Lisa; *Will Smith: A Biography*, Greenwood Biographies, 2009

Jefferson, Alison Rose; *Living the California Dream: African American Leisure Sites during The Jim Crow Era*, University of Nebraska Press, 2022

Knepper, George W.; *Ohio and Its People*, Kent State University Press, 2003

Lear, Norman; *Even This I Get to Experience*, Penguin Books, 2014

Lear, Norman; Colucci, Jim; *All in The Family: The Show That Changed Television*, Universe, 2021

Littlefield, Warren; *Top of the Rock: Inside the Rise and Fall of Must See TV*, Anchor, 2012

Newcomb, Horace; *Encyclopedia of Television*, Fitzroy Dearborn Publisher, 1997

Peisner, David; *Homey Don't Play That! The Story of In Living Color and the Black Comedy Revolution*, 37 Ink, 2018

Schuman, Michael A.; *Will Smith: A Biography of a Rapper Turned Movie Star*, 2013

Bibliography

Smith, Will; Manson, Mark, *Will*, Penguin Press, 2021

Sorin, Gretchen; *Driving While Black*, Liveright, 2020

Tartikoff, Brandon; *The Last Great Ride*, Random House, 1992

Waxman, Sharon; *Rebels on the Backlot*, Harper Collins, 2015

Wikipedia Contributors; *Focus On: 100 Most Popular Television Series by Universal Television*, Focus On, 2017

Wilkerson, Isabel; *The Warmth of Other Suns: The Epic Story of America's Great Migration*, Vintage, 2010

Articles

Andrews-Dyer, Helena, "The story behind Will Smith's iconic 'hug' scene in 'The Fresh Prince of Bel-Air'," *The Washington Post*, September 11, 2020, https://www.washingtonpost.com /arts-entertainment/2020/09/11/fresh-prince-bel-air-hug-father -scene/

Belkin, Lisa, "HARVARD'S GIFTS TO GAG WRITING," *The New York Times*, Monday 29, 1987, https://www.nytimes .com/1987/03/29/arts/harvard-s-gifts-to-gag-writing.html

"BIOGRAPHY OF ALBERT BOROWITZ AND HELEN OS-TERMAN BOROWITZ," Kent State Library, https://www .library.kent.edu/special-collections-and-archives/borowitz -collection-borowitz-biography

Brooks, David, "The Culture of Policing Is Broken," The Atlantic, June 16, 2020, https://www.theatlantic.com/ideas/archive/2020/06 /how-police-brutality-gets-made/613030/

Carter, Bill, "Tartikoff Is Injured in Car Crash," *The New York Times*, January 3, 1991, https://www.nytimes.com/1991/01/03 /arts/tartikoff-is-injured-in-car-crash.html

Carter, Bill, "Brandon Tartikoff, Former NBC Executive Who Transformed TV in the 80's, Dies at 48," *The New York Times*, August 28, 1997, https://www.nytimes.com/1997/08/28/arts /brandon-tartikoff-former-nbc-executive-who-transformed -tv-in-the-80-s-dies-at-48.html

Cerone, Daniel, "A Breath of Fresh Prince: WHY NBC HAS HIGH HOPES ON A RAPPER FROM PHILADELPHIA," *The Los Angeles Times*, July 1, 1990, https://www.latimes.com /archives/la-xpm-1990-07-01-tv-1133-story.html

Chammah, Maurice, "The Real Fresh Prince of Bel-Air Had a

Father in Prison," The Marshall Project, May 6, 2016, https://
www.themarshallproject.org/2016/05/30/the-real-fresh-prince
-of-bel-air-had-a-father-in-prison

Coker, Cheo Hodari, "Good Night, 'Prince'," *The Los Angeles
Times*, May 20, 1996, https://www.latimes.com/archives/la
-xpm-1996-05-20-ca-6351-story.html

Dodson, Aaron; DePaula, Nick, "The 30 best sneakers worn on
'The Fresh Prince of Bel-Air'" The Undefeated, September
10, 2020, https://andscape.com/features/best-sneakers-worn-on
-the-fresh-prince-of-bel-air/

Du Brow, Rick, "NBC's Littlefield Steps Out From Tartikoff's
Shadow: Programming: Entertainment division's No. 2 man
wanted to be No. 1, and got the job. He makes it clear that
he'll be calling the programming shots for the No. 1 network,"
The Los Angeles Times, July 21, 1990, https://www.latimes.com
/archives/la-xpm-1990-07-21-ca-314-story.html

Dunn, Katia, "For Classic TV Producer, Good Times No Longer,"
NPR, July 25, 2006, https://www.npr.org/templates/story/story
.php?storyId=5591655

"Eric Monte: The Writer Who Fought to Change the Stereotypes of
African American in Film!!!" CNN Archives, October 23, 2014,
https://web.archive.org/web/20180310200740/http://ireport.cnn
.com/docs/DOC-1182583

Ford, Andrea, "Actor Ben Vereen Hit by Truck on Highway and Critically Hurt: Accident: He undergoes four hours of surgery for internal and head injuries and a fractured leg after being struck near
his Malibu home," *The Los Angeles Times*, June 10, 1992, https://
www.latimes.com/archives/la-xpm-1992-06-10-me-265-story.html

Gomez, Shirley, "Tatyana Ali Talks Her Journey with Colorism and
Sends A Message To Janet Hubert, *Hola!*, December 15, 2020,
https://www.hola.com/us/celebrities/20211020313034/tatyana
-ali-talks-colorism-janet-hubert/

Gross, Dan, "Will Smith Shouts Out Neighborhood Steak Shop,"
The Philadelphia Inquirer, December 3, 2007, https://www
.inquirer.com/philly/blogs/phillygossip/12076371.html

Hammer, Joshua, "The Fading of The Peacocks," *Newsweek*,
November 8, 1992, https://www.newsweek.com/fading
-peacocks-196802

Bibliography

Harris, Mark, "Will Smith goes to Hollywood," Entertainment Weekly, September 7, 1990, https://ew.com/article/1990/09/07/will-smith-goes-hollywood/

Henderson, Rob, "Everything I Know About Elite America I Learned from 'Fresh Prince' and 'West Wing'", *The New York Times*, October 10, 2020, https://www.nytimes.com/2020/10/10/opinion/sunday/television-culture.html?searchResultPosition=2

Hilburn, Robert, "From the Archives: Striking Tales of Black Frustration and Pride Shake the Pop Mainstream," *The Los Angeles Times*, April 2, 1989, https://www.latimes.com/entertainment/la-et-hilburn-hip-hop-black-1989-link-story.html

Hirschberg, Lynn, "The Lives They Lived: Brandon Tartikoff; Forever 19," *The New York Times*, January 4, 1998, https://www.nytimes.com/1998/01/04/magazine/the-lives-they-lived-brandon-tartikoff-forever-19.html

Horovitz, Bruce, "EVERYBODY WANTS TO GET INTO THE ACT: Support services for screenwriters range from researchers and typists to psychotherapists," *The Los Angeles Times*, October 2, 1989, https://www.latimes.com/archives/la-xpm-1989-10-02-fi-518-story.html

Hough Riots, Wikipedia, https://en.wikipedia.org/wiki/Hough_riots#cite_note-FOOTNOTEHundley1970169-4

Hunter, James, "The Fresh Prince of West Philly turns hip-hop into a love rollercoaster", The Village Voice, December 7, 1999, https://www.villagevoice.com/1999/12/07/the-fresh-prince-of-west-philly-turns-hip-hop-into-a-love-rollercoaster/

Investigation of the Ferguson Police Department, The Justice Department Civil Rights Division, March 4, 2015, https://www.justice.gov/sites/default/files/opa/press-releases/attachments/2015/03/04/ferguson_police_department_report.pdf

James Avery, 1945-2013, Vietnam Veterans of America, https://vva.org/arts-of-war/tv-series/james-avery-1945-2013/

Khal, "Parents Just Don't Understand but Andy Borowitz Gets It," Complex, September 9, 2015, https://www.complex.com/pop-culture/fresh-prince-anniversary-andy-borowitz

Lambert, Craig, "April Fool Every Day," *Harvard Magazine*, May/June 2009, https://www.harvardmagazine.com/2009/05/andy-borowitz

LA Times Archives, "Television IN BRIEF: Tartikoff Gets the Message from Cos," *The Los Angeles Times*, December 8, 1989, https://www.latimes.com/archives/la-xpm-1989-12-08 -ca-284-story.html

LA Times Archives, "Tartikoff and Daughter Hurt in Tahoe Crash," *The Los Angeles Times*, January 3, 1991, https://www .latimes.com/archives/la-xpm-1991-01-03-mn-10617-story.html

Lear, Norman, "Exclusive Norman Lear Memoir Excerpt: Throwdowns with Carroll O'Connor, Race Battles on 'Good Times'," *The Hollywood Reporter*, October 2, 2014, https:// www.hollywoodreporter.com/news/politics-news/norman -lear-memoir-excerpt-throwdowns-736647/

Lee, Chris, "James Avery, 'Fresh Prince' father figure, dies at 65," *The Los Angeles Times*, January 1, 2014, https://www.latimes .com/entertainment/tv/showtracker/la-et-st-james-avery -fresh-prince-father-dies-65-20140101-story.html

McCoy, Terrence, "Ferguson shows how a police force can turn into a plundering 'collection agency'" *The Washington Post*, March 5, 2015, https://www.washingtonpost.com/news/morning -mix/wp/2015/03/05/ferguson-shows-how-a-police-force-can -turn-into-a-plundering-collection-agency/

McFadden, Robert D., "James W. Loewen, Who Challenged How History Is Taught, Dies at 79," *The New York Times*, August 20, 2021, https://www.nytimes.com/2021/08/20/books/james-w -loewen-dead.html

McNamara, Mary, "Column: Inside 'Fresh Prince of Bel-Air' re- union with Joseph Marcell: 'It felt so good to be back'" *The Los Angeles Times*, September 20, 2022, https://www.latimes .com/entertainment-arts/tv/story/2020-09-22/fresh-prince-of -bel-air-reunion-joseph-marcell

Mendoza, N. F., "WITH AN EYE ON . . . : Opposites do attract: Look at Alfonso Ribeiro and 'Fresh Prince's' cousin," *The Los Angeles Times*, June 20, 1993, https://www.latimes.com/archives /la-xpm-1993-06-20-tv-5032-story.html

Mendoza, N. F., "WITH AN EYE ON . . . : Tatyana Ali's 'Fresh Prince' character keeps her grounded," *The Los Angeles Times*, August 21, 1994, https://www.latimes.com/archives /la-xpm-1994-08-21-tv-29427-story.html

Bibliography

Mitchell, John, "Plotting His Next Big Break," *The Los Angeles Times*, April 14, 2006, https://www.latimes.com/archives/la -xpm-2006-apr-14-me-monte14-story.html

Nodjimbadem, Katie, "The Lesser-Known History of African-American Cowboys," Smithsonianmag.com, February 13, 2017, https://www.smithsonianmag.com/history/lesser-known-history -african-american-cowboys-180962144/

O'Connor, Meg, "La Paz Cop Who Pulled Over Black Man for Air Freshener Is Fired," *Phoenix New Times*, March 5, 2020, https:// www.phoenixnewtimes.com/news/black-man-pulled -over-driving-with-air-freshener-la-paz-arizona-11453861

Parker, Lyndsey, "David Foster opens up about Ben Vereen car accident, Kat McPhee marriage and superstar career," yahoo!, July 1, 2020, https://www.yahoo.com/now/david-foster-opens -up-about-ben-vereen-car-accident-kat-mc-phee-marriage -and-superstar-career-212500308.html

Pearce, Matt; Srikrishnan, Maya; Zucchin, David, "Protesters and Police Face Off in St. Louis Suburb Over Shooting," *The Los Angeles Times*, August 11, 2014, https://www.latimes.com/nation /nationnow/la-na-missouri-st-louis-police-shooting-teen -20140811-story.html#page=1

Perry, Armon, "The reality of Black men's love lives and marriages is very different than what's usually shown on TV—I spent years actually talking to them," The Conversation, December 16, 2020, https://theconversation.com/the-reality-of-black-mens -love-lives-and-marriages-is-very-different-than-whats-usually -shown-on-tv-i-spent-years-actually-talking-to-them-151166

Persaud, Christine, "The Fresh Prince of Bel-Air: How Old the Cast Was During Season 1 Vs Now," Screen Rant, December 6, 2020, https://screenrant.com/fresh-prince-of-bel-air-main-cast-ages/

Raab, Scott, "Will Smith on Kids, His Career, Ferguson, and Failure," *Esquire*, February 12, 2015, https://www.esquire.com /entertainment/interviews/a9938/will-smith-interview-0315/

Reid, Joe, "The Enduring Legacy of Norman Lear's *Good Times*," Primetimer, December 16, 2019, https://www.primetimer.com /features/everything-you-need-to-know-about-good-times

Reilly, Sue, "Ex-Aunt Vivian Has Her Own Studio and a Little Fresh Prince," The Los Angeles Times, August 23, 1993,

https://www.latimes.com/archives/la-xpm-1993-08-23-me
-27099-story.html

Rohter, James, "'Fresh Prince of Bel Air' Puts Rap in Mainstream," *The New York Times*, September 17, 1990, https://www.ny
times.com/1990/09/17/arts/fresh-prince-of-bel-air-puts-rap
-in-mainstream.html

Rothenberg, Fred, "NBC in the '80s: From Worst to First Part IV: Tartikoff Tot Starts 'Cosby Show' Rolling for," AP News, April 16, 1986, https://apnews.com/article/de944a090a6343135a76374
6ce8b5031

Saenz, Arlette, "Eric Holder: Justice Dept. 'Prepared' to Dismantle Ferguson Police Dept. If 'Necessary'" ABC News, March 6, 2015, https://abcnews.go.com/Politics/eric-holder-justice-dept
-prepared-dismantle-ferguson-police/story?id=29454592

Saperstein, Pat, "'The Fresh Prince of Bel-Air' Writer Andy Borowitz on Rappers and Retiring from TV," *Variety*, August 19, 2015, https://variety.com/2015/tv/news/fresh-prince-of-bel-air
-will-smith-andy-borowitz-1201570488/

"Tartikoff and Other Motorist Share Blame for New Year's Day Accident," AP News, February 9, 1991, https://apnews.com
/article/cd7ccf9acd381084ae8713d81fa5cf21

The Associated Press, "Broadway Star Not Dead," Lakeland Ledger, June 5, 1984, https://news.google.com/newsp
apers?nid=1346&dat=19840605&id=qLYwAAAAIBAJ
&pg=3789,2179141

"The Negro Motorist Green Book, Wikipedia, https://
en.wikipedia.org/wiki/The_Negro_Motorist_Green_Book

Tinsley, Justin, "Uncle Phil from 'The Fresh Prince of Bel-Air' may be the best TV dad in history—this scene proves it," The Undefeated, June 15, 2018, https://andscape.com/features
/uncle-phil-from-the-fresh-prince-of-bel-air-may-be-the-best
-tv-dad-in-history-this-scene-proves-it/

Topel, Fred, "Will Smith Shocked 'Fresh Prince of Bel-Air' Uncle Phil Actor James Avery with His Hidden Talent," cheatsheet.com, November 19, 2021, https://www.cheatsheet
.com/entertainment/will-smith-shocked-fresh-prince-of-bel
-air-uncle-phil-james-avery-hidden-talent.html/

Trex, Ethan, "5 Things You Didn't Know About Quincy Jones,"

Mental Floss, March 12, 2010, https://www.mentalfloss.com /article/24191/5-things-you-didnt-know-about-quincy-jones

Walsh, Sean Collins, "Driving While Black," *The Philadelphia Inquirer*, October 14, 2021, https://www.inquirer.com/news /philadelphia-city-council-isaiah-thomas-police-driving -while-black-20211014.html

Waxman, Olivia, "The *Fresh Prince* Turns 25: The Show's Creators on Will Smith, Reboots and Race," *Time*, September 10, 2015, https://time.com/4021944/quincy-jones-borowitz-fresh-prince -bel-air-anniversary/

"Will Smith, 1986," MIT Archives, https://www.blackhistory.mit .edu/archive/will-smith-1986

Wojciechowski, Michele, "The Lawlessness of Andy Borowitz," *Parade*, November 7, 2016, https://parade.com/521931 /michelewojciechowski/the-lawlessness-of-andy-borowitz/

Yates, Clinton, "Donald Glover, Issa Rae, Baratunde Thurston: The rise of the black nerd?" *The Washington Post*, November 26, 2012, https://www.washingtonpost.com/blogs/therootdc /post/donald-glover-issa-rae-baratunde-thurston-the-rise -of-the-black-nerd/2012/11/26/7015b27e-37dd-11e2-a263 -f0ebffed2f15_blog.html

Zeman, Ned, "Will Smith Rides High," *Vanity Fair*, July 1999, https://archive.vanityfair.com/article/1999/7/will-smith-rides -high

Videos

"1991 Will Smith interview," The Arsenio Hall Show, https://www .youtube.com/watch?v=YEaTF7bqHsM

"Alfonso Ribeiro—Not Too Young (To Fall In Love)" Alfonso Ribeiro, https://www.youtube.com/watch?v=VsCED5mLuKY

"Alfonso Ribeiro Talks About His Dancing Skills," BUILD Series, December 28, 2017, https://www.youtube.com /watch?v=jbq9YHndM-4

"Driving While Black: Race, Space, and Mobility in America," PBS, October 13, 2020, https://www.pbs.org/video/driving -while-black-race-space-and-mobility-in-america-achvfr/

"Film School NYFA—Guest Lecture—James Avery Part 1," New

York Film Academy, June 2007, https://www.youtube.com
/watch?v=Fc6d_wBCU6c

"FRESH PRINCE OF BEL-AIR Panel—Wizard World Virtual
Experiences 2020," Fandom Spotlite, September 18, 2020,
https://www.youtube.com/watch?v=dueXFfPAEvU

"How I Became The Fresh Prince of Bel-Air | STORYTIME,"
Will Smith, https://www.youtube.com/watch?v=y_WoOYybCro

"If You Only Knew: Alfonso Ribeiro," Larry King Now, November
2, 2018, https://www.youtube.com/watch?v=huBoPA7srgc&t=4s

"Interview with James Avery," blogtalkradio, https://www.youtube
.com/watch?v=eAvg64Wel4s

"Janet Hubert, original Aunt Viv of 'Fresh Prince,' opens up
about Will Smith's apology and more," Eyewitness News
ABC7 NY, December 13, 2020, https://www.youtube.com
/watch?v=qcboazD-PW8&t=632s

"Joseph Marcell AKA "Geoffrey" Gets Emotional Remembering His
FINAL MOMENTS With James Avery!" Viral Hip Hop News,
September 2020, https://www.youtube.com/watch?v=x-Fsq0SD
-iw&list=PL83giuXKQ33wXuowVJ_4gVGt5mV3x44YM

"Joseph Marcell On Growing Up In The SLUMS Of London The
Fresh Prince Janet Hubert James Avery & More," Viral Hip
Hop News, November 27, 2020, https://www.youtube.com
/watch?v=Bpe6X5yH1eI

"Lord Hummingbird—Teenage Bossa Nova Girl" Lord Hummingbird, https://www.youtube.com/watch?v=_hZzu6DiiK4

"Lori Openden Casting Executive," Television Academy Founda-
tion, February 6, 2020, https://www.youtube.com
/watch?v=8AYoNaKCP3k&t=474s

"Will Smith Interview about Fresh Prince," The Tonight Show
with Jay Leno, July 14, 2017, https://www.youtube.com
/watch?v=kRaXTgntjdo

"Will Smith The Fresh Prince freestyle 1989—Westwood,"
TimWestwoodTV, https://www.youtube.com/watch?
v=M2vJZUZL3pw

"Winifred Hervey on working with Will Smith on "The Fresh
Prince of Bel-Air," FoundationINTERVIEWS, March 15, 2016,
https://www.youtube.com/watch?v=ck8yQ1HeC2Q

Bibliography

Other Media

A Different World Complete Series, 1987-1993

All in the Family: The Complete Series, 1971-1979

Family Ties The Complete Series, 1982-1989

Good Times—The Complete Series, 1974-1979

In Living Color—The Complete Series, 1990-1994

Martin—The Complete Series, 1992-1997

Maude: The Complete Series, 1972-1978

The Cosby Show—The Complete Series, 1984-1992

The Fresh Prince of Bel-Air, The Complete Series, 1990-1996

The Fresh Prince of Bel-Air Episode Guide, IMDb
    https://www.imdb.com/title/tt0098800/episodes

The Fresh Prince of Bel-Air, Episode Ninja
    https://episode.ninja/series/the-fresh-prince-of-bel-air

The Jeffersons: The Complete Series—The Dee-luxe Edition,
    1975-1985

Smell you later.

INDEX

Note: "WS" refers to the actor Will Smith, and "AB" refers to Andy Borowitz. "Will" refers to the character Will Smith in *Fresh Prince*.

Index

Index

Index

Index

Index

AUTHOR'S NOTE

The stories contained within this book have been gathered over the course of a year and include original firsthand interviews with many involved in the production, including creators Andy and Susan Borowitz and many actors, producers, writers, directors, and industry insiders.

I drew on more than two hundred published articles, interviews, videos, and podcasts. To understand the *Fresh Prince* universe required multiple viewings of all 148 episodes of *The Fresh Prince of Bel-Air* to break down, analyze, and process the triumphs, failures, hopes, and dreams of my pretend family.

I spent hundreds of hours viewing both Black sitcoms and otherwise of the last six decades to place myself in the world that led to *The Fresh Prince of Bel-Air*.

ABOUT THE AUTHOR

CHRIS PALMER is a longtime sportswriter who has covered the National Basketball Association and culture for twenty-five years for *ESPN The Magazine* and all of ESPN's digital platforms. He's contributed to ESPN's *The Undefeated*, *Bleacher Report*, *GQ* and *Slam*, as well as various other outlets. He's authored six books, including *New York Times* bestsellers *Wide Open*, the autobiography of Supercross Champion Jeremy McGrath, and former Laker great Lamar Odom's memoir *Darkness To Light*. He lives in Los Angeles.